My Peace, My Soul... Can't Be Bought or Sold

This comfort you too can hold

Printed in the United States of America.

Packaged by WinePress Publishing, PO Box 428, Enumclaw, WA 98022. The views expressed or implied in this work do not necessarily reflect those of WinePress Publishing. Ultimate design, content, and editorial accuracy of this work is the responsibility of the author.

ISBN 1-57921-352-9
Library of Congress Catalog Card Number: 00-111305

Foreword

It is through life's deepest experiences I am called to share with you the fact that God truly loves you. It is the desire of my heart to share words of encouragement and hope, filling you with joy, peace and love. All freely given from God above, simply a radiation of His unconditional love.

Through a vast array of experiences in my own life, times of great burden and periods of joyful bliss, from one extreme to the other, I wandered alone. Suddenly, I ended up with such a messed up life that I prayed tomorrow would never come. Admittedly, I never sought the will of my Father. As it turns out, where else would I rather turn? No place!!

God gives me words of encouragement each day and I want to share them with you. I had to hit *Rock Bottom,* as they say in the country, lying on my back with no view of anything other than straight up, before I truly sought God's love for me. Hopefully, you won't have to wait until you hit *Rock Bottom* before you look up. However, if you are like most of us, so near-sighted we can't see beyond today, this message of God's unconditional love is for you.

Jesus Christ, God's only Son, my personal Savior, brings great comfort and joy to me, just knowing that He is always there. Guess what? That means we are never alone! You may already know this. If so, you are truly blessed. Unfortunately, many people have never been introduced to this Security. That is why I feel compelled to share The Father, Son and Holy Spirit, my Eternal Life "Security Blanket" with you. What a blessed gift of love sent from God above!

It is my prayer that every single word serves as a blessing to you in whatever you are experiencing right now in your life.

May God Bless You in His Own Special and Bountiful Way.

In Jesus Name I Pray.

I am doing what The Father told me to do.
I am just sharing my blessings with you.

—Suzan Dickinson
Edmond, Oklahoma

Psalm 40:1–5 (NIV)

I waited patiently for the Lord; he turned to me and heard my cry. He lifted me out of the Slimy pit, out of the mud and mire, he set my feet on a rock and gave me a firm place to stand. He put a new song in my mouth, a hymn of praise to our God. Many will see and fear and put their trust in the Lord. Blessed is the man who makes the Lord his trust, who does not look to the proud, to those who turn aside to false gods. Many, O Lord my God, are the wonders you have done. The things you planned for us no one can recount to you; were I to speak and tell of them, they would be too many to declare.

Acknowledgments

Thank You, Heavenly Father for the gift of Eternal Life and Inspirational Poetry.
And for my beautiful children, Candice, Gabrielle, John, and Andrew who are perfect gifts from you.

A special thanks to the earthly father of my children, Dr. W. Paul Dickinson, for his belief in me.

To my parents who always allowed me to be me. Thank you for raising me in God's House and in His Word. Those two factors have been the prevailing forces throughout my life.

Thank you
To my Pastor, Dr. Alan Day and his lovely wife, Alice, who truly live exemplary lives.

Thanks
To my family and friends who have prayerfully supported me in this endeavor.

Last, but not least, a tribute to my grandmother, the late Elva Voyles, who taught me to live by faith in truth and to work hard, all of which she did. She was the most content person I have ever known, all of which is contributed to her unwavering faith in Jesus Christ, the Son of God.

While I was in Washington signing the contract for this book, my children's father Dr. Dickinson and I talked, and I read the acknowledgment to him and he wept for joy, while telling the children during our phone conversation. Only hours later, he suffered a massive stroke and departed this life just ten days later.

Book Description

If you have spent your life searching for something, not sure of just what you were in search of, this book will aide you on the destiny of your soul's journey.

Love, Joy, Peace, and comfort are the most sought after commodities in life.

May you find great comfort in the revealing of God's Love, giving you inner peace, accompanied with an abundance of Joy.

In our life, we face and are challenged by many trials and failures. God's gift to me, a healing process in the form of poetry. Healing is an essential step that must accompany each one of our disappointments in life. This gift has been instrumental in my own life.

The poetry in this book is a gift from God, one meant for sharing. Our life must maintain balance and keep focused on the things that are good in order to carry on. This poetry is filled with inspiration, rhythm and rhyme to aide in the balance that is needed for our journey in this chaotic world while pressing forward to our final destination.

Psalm 147:3 (NIV)

He heals the brokenhearted and binds up their wounds.

Contents

Psalms 62:1–2 (NIV)
My soul finds rest in God alone: My salvation comes from him. He alone is my rock and my salvation; he is my fortress, I will never be shaken.

Psalm 23

The Lord is my shepherd; I shall not want. He maketh me to lie down in green pastures: he leadeth me beside the still waters. He restoreth my soul: he leadeth me in the paths of righteousness for his name's sake. Yea, though I walk through the valley of the shadow of death, I will fear no evil: for thou art with me; thy rod and thy staff they comfort me. Thou preparest a table before me in the presence of mine enemies: thou anointest my head with oil; my cup runneth over. Surely goodness and mercy shall follow me all the days of my life: and I will dwell in the house of the Lord forever.

Entertain Strangers

Many people and events will touch our life.
However, there is no individual or event like the touch of one life.
The life of Jesus Christ touches the lives of millions each day,
Always in a unique, and positive way.

Many individuals come and go.
Most of them, we do not know.
Jesus wants to touch them in a positive way.
So, we must not fail to share the story of Jesus along the way.

Make a plan each day to pray for God's way.
So when we see someone down,
let us reach out in love and pray,
Allowing God to bless them in His own special way.
Why would we fail to share His love,
with anyone we meet today?

Hebrews 13:2

Be not forgetful to entertain strangers: for thereby some have entertained angels unaware.

Mind's Eye View

Majestic is the mind's eye view
Just picturing the grand presence of being with You.

The mind just races away at the thought.
Salvation for our soul has already been bought.

Such a price God did pay. Who else was sinless enough to redeem?
God knew He had to outweigh the son of perdition's evil scheme.

Giving His one and only sin-free son,
To accomplish the redemptive mission,
For He was The Only One.

We all have our own mission for God's Kingdom to do.
Are you willing or do you think it's for
someone other than you?

My Dear Friend, you better think again.
The time has come for your mission to begin.

Ask The Father what He wants you to do.
He will point you in a direction, that seems all new.

That's exactly what He wanted to do,
Letting you know it's not you, it is He that will lead you.

You will always be aware that you had no strength prior.
That is exactly The Father's Will and desire.

It is very bizarre, but He will set you on fire,
All just to carry out the mission of His own desire.

Get ready to serve, for we all have a mission,
Just waiting for our submission.

2 Thessalonians 3:5 (NIV)

May the Lord direct your hearts into God's love and Christ's perseverance.

Our Inheritance

The knowledge of who we are in Christ sometimes gets
unconsciously jostled about.
We may temporarily lose consciousness from time to time until
danger lurks about.
Then we give a fearful shout, "Oh Dear God, please help me
I need you now, no doubt!"
We instantly imagine we're in the midst of a subconscious illusion.
No way! It is suddenly revealed it's our Heavenly Father
beyond any misconception and it's conclusion.
No, you are not suffering a concussion,
not even the smallest bit of confusion.
You are becoming more aware of your inheritance.
It is of crucial timing for you and your gift's acceptance.
You automatically become an heir through redemption, and
there is no time for reluctance.
Your Heavenly Father gave you alone 6000 Angels, one for
every moment Twenty-Four—Seven.
All you must do is call unto your Heavenly Father
which art in Heaven.
Your band of Angels that was assigned you are
miraculously in direct flight straight from Heaven,
Giving you protection from the evil one.
You are no longer in fear's captivity.
So, Dear Heir, enjoy this reality. It's yours throughout all Eternity.

Joshua 1:9

Have I not commanded thee? Be strong and of a good courage: be not afraid, neither be thou dismayed: for the Lord thy God is with thee whithersoever thou goest.

Right Direction

Even when I don't know the way,
You will always point me in the right direction;

Giving me all the right connections.
Always, with Your loving affection.

Protecting me all the way,
Father, it sure makes for a great day!

Your connections, always come at the most crucial time.
Most usually, when I haven't a dime!

That's Grace Divine!
Especially, after Praying, Father Your will, not mine.

Psalms 121:8 (NIV)

The Lord will watch over your coming and going both now and forevermore.

Faithful to the End

You're forever faithful to the end.
It's on you I can always depend!
It was You that removed me from living my life in sin.

You're so loving and so kind,
Your love simply blows my Mind!
I'm so happy in your word,
I have found truth in all I've heard.

Thank You Father God,
For being ever faithful to the end!

Isaiah 48:16

Come ye near unto me, hear ye this; I have not spoken in secret from the beginning; from that time that it was, there I am; and now the Lord, God, and His Spirit, hath sent me.

Repay

There is no earthly way for us to repay,
God's gift of eternal life,
but we can share with others His blessings each day.

We can start by telling over and over His awesome story,
And tell all about His only Son Jesus,
Our Savior, whom God sent from glory.

We must not forget to tell all those whom we meet,
how they, too, can turn from their sin,
How they, too, can dedicate their life to Him.

This will allow them to join in telling the awesome story,
While on their journey from Earth to glory.

Father, thank You for the blessings You send each day.
Your blessings sure make life's journey sweeter, day by day!

Proverbs 10:21 (NIV)
The lips of the righteous nourish many, but fools die for lack of judgment.

Liberated

Must ye feel the need to be liberated?

Be ye liberated from the grasp of Satan's hold.
Ye must realize that Satan's grip is the grip of death, unlike Christ's hold.

Must ye be reminded that Satan tried to grasp hold of Jesus?

Jesus did not give him anything to grasp hold of,
For the Son knew what His Father was made of.

Jesus had one hand up in praise to His Father.

The other grasping tightly to His Father's hand,
Leaving Satan to stand alone on sinking sand.

Ye must not let go of the Father's hand.

Tell Satan not to even bother, for his death grip has been banned.
Now that ye are protected by the blood of the Lamb.

Praises be unto God! For ye are liberated from Satan's death hold!

Proverbs 15:21b
A man of understanding walketh uprightly.

Crimson Flood

Jesus lives in me
For all the world to see.
I have nothing to give,
Nothing I own,
Be it rags or riches.
They're not fit for a throne.
The sins of my forefathers and me,
He did not condone.
But, for all of us,
Our Savior on the tree did groan!

He bled and died on Calvary's Hill
To give us Eternal life
And the forgiveness of sins.
At His Father's request, He followed His will.

The image remains in my head
Every night when I go to bed.
It wasn't just a single drop
Of His Precious blood
He bled,
But, for all of our sins.
It was the "Crimson Flood"
That cleansed us clean,
Now and forever our sins can no longer be seen.

Ephesians 1:7
In whom we have redemption through His blood, the forgiveness of sins, according to the riches of His grace.

Take My Life

Father, you made the heavens and the earth in seven short days.
Please take my life and sculpt it with Your masterful ways.

Help me keep my mind on You.
When occasions arise to stray; please show me
what it is You want me to do.

Make me ever so mindful of You and Your ways,
Making my life full of continuous praise.

When giving praise to You, my heart is filled
with overflowing joy,
Making me totally aware my life is not a toy.

Father, Your Holy Spirit allows me
to recognize Satan's deceitful ploys;
In his attempts he no longer confuses,
for the Holy Spirit blocks his annoys.

Colossians 3:2 (NIV)
Set your mind on things above, not on earthly things.

Character

Consistent

Is your spiritual life consistent?
Do you permit sin to grow in your life, becoming to God's Will resistant?

God allows us many opportunities and time to share.
Our spare time should be spent letting the lost know
God really does care.

Being consistent is your commitment to God.
His commitment to us is always giving us strength to resist what's odd.

Your prayer time is a must.
How else could you ever in Him, place your trust?

Reading His Word everyday
Gives you the wisdom to help you on your way.

Following the Golden Rule
With all of the above leaves you no need for any other tool.

My Dear Friend, that is mighty cool!
In other words, if you are consistent in your spiritual life, you're no fool!

Luke 12:43
Blessed is that servant, whom his lord when cometh shall find so doing.

The Master's Tool

Father, please remove all carnal thoughts for they try to rule.
Please allow The Holy Spirit to use my life as "The Master's tool."

I pray that my emotional life that is full of desire ceases,
Halting the force of rebellion of God's Will
so that my spiritual life increases;

The only turbulence I want to experience is the act of The Holy Spirit
Reshaping and preparing my life, for His service, then declare it!

Father, I pray this in The Precious Name of Your Son Jesus,
To glorify You, Father, and Your Kingdom, for it is Your Son who frees us.

Matthew 5:16
Let your light so shine before men, that they may see your good works, and glorify your Father which is in heaven.

Simple Reflection

Sent in direct flow, from heaven above.
The river of life reflects our Dear Savior's love.

Still bodies of water reflect an image of what's above.
Would your reflection be one of hate or love?

This will let you know, if you're headed in the right direction;
Or, If your soul is in need of Divine protection?

It is amazing what can be seen in a simple reflection.
Thank God, for our souls Divine protection.

Proverbs 27:19 (NIV)
As water reflects a face, so a man's heart reflects the man.

All Grown

Painfully aware of the years gone by,
We ask ourselves, where did the years fly?

It seems just yesterday when they arrived.
Looking back at the memories, we even wonder how we survived?

The first smile, word, crawl, and step,
Now we just wish for half that pep.

There were many more first's that have occurred,
Some of them we would all agree were a little absurd.

Now as we glow in awe of what we observe,
For we all know there were times we did not give them
what they deserved.

The struggles we faced in the past,
Brush your teeth, make your bed, clean your room,
those are gone at last.

Wait a minute, oh no, my baby is now grown!
The bags are packed for college, now they will be on their own.

All grown up!

Proverbs 22:6 (NIV)
Train a child in the way he should go, and when he is old he will not turn from it.

Perfect Example

Our children need a perfect example,
Always knowing there is nothing else ample.
If you have never had one,
And don't know one,
Allow me to introduce you to my Heavenly Father.
Oh no, it won't be a bother.
My Heavenly Father sets High standards.
He is our Perfect Example.
He left us a complex sample,
Detailing the Perfect Example.
First you must read and believe,
That He is the Supplier of all your needs.
And that through Him, all sins are relieved!
That's factual. It is in His Book, Don't forget the title,
"The Holy Bible"!

1 Timothy 4:12

Let no man despise thy youth; But be thou an example of the believers, in word, in conversation, in charity, in spirit, in faith, in purity.

His Father's Will

COMMITMENT

God's Son, Jesus, had no ambition of His own.
Doing His Father's Will was most important.
A great deal of the time He felt alone.

Jesus, a kind and compassionate man,
gave His love for all to receive.
Jesus joyfully accepts the sinner in repentance.
Salvation is the fulfillment of our greatest need.

Jesus died like a criminal, as did the lowly,
Staked to a cross even though He was sinless and in truth,
He was God's one and only.

Jesus could have called for thousands of Angels to assist Him.
But He resisted His own desire for physical relief;
all while the crowd mocked Him.

They were spitting at Him and shouting, "where is your God?"
They were not able to understand His love for His Father.
To the lost, seemed a bit odd.

They did not know He was carrying out the Will of His Father.
He was dying for the salvation of all.
Jesus knew, so the Angels He did not bother.

He was doing His Father's Will.
To you and I, that seems unreal.

He, God's child, carrying out His Father's Will
so all could receive salvation through Him.
We are all God's children. We, too, must seek The Father's Will.

Psalms 40:8
I delight to do thy will, O my God: yea, thy law is within my heart.

Communion

The Master Calleth

It's time for a fine Dining experience with "The Heavenly Host."
It is the most sophisticated form of dining served with a toast.

You must never forget,
"The Heavenly Host" has personally invited you.
Allow Him the opportunity to redeem,
giving to you spiritual life anew.

The only way you can dine with Him
is by searching your soul for unforgiven sin.
You must pray a prayer of repentance.
This is the only way you can dine with Him.

In repentance, you have now put away the former things.
The previous manner of nature is now gone
with departure of sin. Oh, such joy it brings!

After receiving Christ as your Savior,
The Word of God says ye must be baptized.
You were chosen by God, He is delighted you finally realized.

The main course is bread. It represents "The Body of Christ."
The toast is with wine. It represents "The Blood of Christ."

Do this all in the remembrance of Christ.
If, for any other reason, you better think twice.

If you partake of "The Body Of Christ" in a guilty manner,
You might as well wear a death banner.

Dining with "The Heavenly Host" is by judgment
of a God given personal conviction.
Thank God for His Son's Body, Blood,
and The Holy Spirit all for our redemption.

The Master Calleth, so come and dine.
Partake of the bread, and toast with the wine.

You are His Chosen guest.
You Are The Branches and He Is The Vine.

The Master Calleth, so come quickly, come and dine!

1 Corinthians 11:24–25
And when he had given thanks, he brake it, and said, "Take, eat: this is my body, which is broken for you: this do in remembrance of me." After the same manner also he took the cup, when he had supped, saying, "This cup is the new testament in my blood: this do ye, as oft as ye drink it, in remembrance of me."

Confession

Do not listen to the great deceiver.
It is to The Lord you must be a pleaser.
When The Holy Spirit falls upon you,
You better get down on your knees.
Ask The Father to help you, please!
He wants a sincere heart
That's without deception.
He expects a full "Confession"
About the sins you have committed.
He will forgive and forget,
And for you, there will be no regret.
Stay in His Word each and every day,
He will lead and guide you on your way.
You must not forget to pray,
Paying full respect to The Father, Son and Holy Spirit.

Romans 10:10

For with the heart man believeth unto righteousness; and with the mouth confession is made unto salvation.

We All Have a Cross

We all have our cross to bear.
Many of us unaware, that God really does care.

This is exactly why God sent Jesus.
He is the only one who can free us.

Our cross may be a bodily affliction or chemical addiction.
He can set us free through spiritual redemption.

He is our intercessor,
If to Him we are a sin confessor.

Until we fully give it up, ever increasing is sin and it's pressure.
All from Satan and his demons, in our business, he is a Messer.

Your soul at birth was God-given.
But if you've placed your faith in self, that is all self-driven.

If your faith is placed anywhere other than in Christ,
My dear one, it is time for you to be born twice.

Job 5:7–9

Yet man is born to trouble, as the sparks fly upward. I would seek unto God, and unto God would I commit my cause: Which doeth great things and unsearchable; marvelous things without number.

Don't Risk It

Direction

We must not let our Bible become dusty,
For that is what causes God's commands in our mind to become rusty.

We are taught very early in life,
that when rust builds on metal, it will break.
Breaking God's commands would be spiritual death,
a risk we cannot afford to take.

God's commands must be fresh in our mind.
Staying fresh in our mind is God's way
of keeping us out of a sinful bind.

The commands of God keep our minds in square frame.
All of which keeps us from feeling guilty and going insane.

When we follow God's commands
we will never become spiritually lame!

Romans 8:6

For to be carnally minded is death; but to be spiritually minded is life and peace.

Being Equipped

No longer constantly suppressing desires.
Too busy seeking to find out what the mission requires.

It is in our suffering, we are being equipped to serve.
Telling the heartbroken, sick and afflicted
about the Love of Jesus, for it's unheard.

We all have crosses to bear, we need not dilute.
For the very crosses we bear, when pruned by God,
is what produces good fruit.

Immediately freed by the Spirit of God.
By the acceptance of the cross, we are no longer at odd.

Make Haste!
Don't make your life on this earth The Kingdom's Waste!

Psalms 38:9
Lord, all my desire is before thee; And my groaning is not hid from thee.

Don't Wait Too Late

No matter the depth of hurt and bitterness left from love
given in the past,

We must accept God's love, for it is the best and it will forever last.

So very petty and selfish is the sinful one's love,
Precious, innocent, and forgiving like a child
is the awesome Love of God from above.

The sinful one's love and life had many limitations!
Acceptance of Jesus, God's Son, with forgiveness granted,
God's love has no limitations.

As the sinful one recognizes no pleasure
in the physical birth, for all are sinners born,
He is reminded by the Holy Spirit his need to be reborn.

Don't hesitate when you recognize the revelation.
Why on Earth, would one wait too late?
For it is the coming of God that happens in an instant,
and we do not know the time or date!

Titus 3:3–4 (NIV)

At one time we too were foolish, disobedient, deceived and enslaved by all kinds of passions and pleasures. We lived in malice and envy, being hated and hating one another. But when the kindness and love of God our Savior appeared, He saved us, not because of righteous things we had done, but because of His mercy. He saved us through the washing of rebirth and renewal by the Holy Spirit, whom He poured out on us generously through Jesus Christ our Savior, so that, having been justified by His grace, we might become heir having the hope of eternal life.

Destructive Brew

Do not drink from the bitter cup of wrath.
Oh, it is such a destructive brew.
Filled with sin and strife, heartache is all it serves you.

Disappointment is what's in it and it's filled to the brim,
Making your future so very bleak and dim.
God sent His Son to die for our sin.

Since God sent His Son to die for our sin.
Don't you think it's about time to get in touch with Him?
Just go to your knees asking forgiveness please.

He is the drink called Eternal Life.
He is the drink that removes all bitterness and strife.

He melts away all the pain of your past.
Giving you Joy, Hope, Peace and Love that will eternally last!

Leviticus 10:10

And that ye may put difference between holy and unholy; and between unclean and clean.

Faith in Action

Don't waste your life's precious time
worrying and wondering about what's next!
For if you do, you will be taking God's plans
for your life out of context.

Plan your day with others in mind.
Jesus was not concerned about Himself, but all mankind.

God planned for us to find satisfaction,
without being a part of Satan's distractions!
But to live out His plan, we must put our faith in action.

Faith is trusting and believing,
all of which takes less energy
Than doubting and unbelieving,
all of which comes from our enemy.

Satan sneaks in little by little,
All attempts are just to belittle.

Satan would even lead us to believe we are in control.
We might even follow along for a while, until Jesus reminds us
He has already paid the toll.

Letting us know God the Father is in control,
And the toll He paid is what gives eternal life to our lost soul!

Faith is a small act to put into action,
When we know God the Father is the main attraction!

Hebrews 11:1
Faith is the substance of things hoped for, the evidence of things not seen.

Boaster

Go for it! Enjoy being a success boaster.
However, during the boasting process,
you're becoming a spiritual coaster.

Don't be satisfied with your career full of success,
But continually seek God's will for your life, and God will bless.

You're furthering God's Kingdom when spreading His Word
By simply telling the poor and lonely, He died to become their Lord.

In sharing The Faith they learn about Forgiveness.
Just by being available for forgiveness brings forth their righteousness.
It is Impossible for all to enter God's Kingdom.
All who desire to enter must Turn from evil,
and turn to God to reach your
soul's freedom.
Now Dear Friend you are Heaven Bound!

Galatians 2:20–21 (NIV)
I have been crucified with Christ and I no longer live, but Christ lives in me. The life I live in body, I live by faith in the Son of God, who loved me and gave himself for me. I do not set aside the grace of God, for if righteousness could be gained through the law, Christ died for nothing!

Faith

Living in the sensorial realm is merely living in the flesh.
All five senses allow Satan tools for deception, putting faith to test.

Time in God's Word gives Wisdom and Faith sufficient for any test.
For this achievement, God promises us we will be blessed.

Remaining in the state of depression allows spiritual regression.
Depression is primarily caused by sins, not given to confession.

Doing God's Will does not always bring immediate pleasure.
Jesus was crucified, that is end's length in pain's measure.

However, our willingness to serve Him
Blesses us with a mansion in Glory. Oh, that is a victorious win.

No more awful test to face, Satan failed God's redemption quest.
My Dear Friend, living by Faith puts the sensorial realm to rest.

Assurance of Heaven based on feelings is spiritual death.
Assurance of Heaven is received by Faith.

Hebrews 10:22
Let us draw near with a true heart in full assurance of faith, having our hearts sprinkled from an evil conscience, and our bodies washed with pure water.

Unfamiliarity

Leap out in faith into the place of unfamiliarity.
God will show you great and mighty things with all clarity.
You must put away that apathetic attitude.
It is about time to display true gratitude.
God uses all of us from conception to death,
Before we are formed in the womb, until we draw our last breath.
It is the broken and desperate, He heals and seeks to lift,
Instantly filling with spiritual gifts, amazingly healing so swift.
Never forget, it is the low in this life He chooses to use.
When He saves and touches their life, they had nothing to lose.
When things are going your way and your pockets are deep,
Isn't it amazing, we lose no sleep?
Remember, the things in this world are not ours to keep.
So, when pondering what next to buy, think about lost sheep.
Sharing our Faith in The Shepherd with His lost sheep,
Gives them the Faith they need to leap.

Matthew 17:20

And Jesus said unto them, Because of your unbelief: for verily I say unto you, if ye have faith as a grain of mustard seed, ye shall say unto this mountain, Remove hence to yonder place; and it shall remove; and nothing shall be impossible unto you.

Brush Up On Your History

When you doubt the victory,
You better brush up on your history.
God destroyed those who chose not to follow Him;
He needed a few good fishers of men,
To seek the lost, for the forgiveness of sin,
To tell them to stay on the path,
And not to do it all again!

Much of this world has a battle yet to win,
Brothers and sisters let us begin
Showing them the way it all began.

It was Jesus, in such a short life span,
That completed His Father's command.
He traveled about the land,
He with The Master, hand and hand.
From His Birth, Death and Resurrection,
No one can understand the completion.
But by faith measuring as tiny as a mustard seed,
My Dear Friend, He will always succeed!

Hebrews 11:30 (NIV)

By faith the walls of Jericho fell, after the people had marched round them.

Mother

Proverbs 31:28 (NIV)
Her children arise up, and call her Blessed.
Her husband, also, and he praiseth her.

The definition of the word "MOTHER" has yet to meet
the true definition.
God needed a way on earth to extend His Love.
That is why Mothers have hearts and hugs big enough
to extend much love,
A special gift from God above . . .

. . To my Mother. .

No words can describe the love that you give.
There is no other like to discover as long as I live.

The love you give your children, No lyrics put to tune.
The music yet written could match such an heirloom.

Every day you go beyond the call,
Not to just one, but to all.

Mom, I love and appreciate you more, and more each day.
Never realizing, how much I would cherish just listening to you pray.

God Bless You . . .

Little Guy

Have you ever told anyone about Jesus?
Oh, Father, Please forgive us.
In your death, from our sins, You freed us.

I know You are displeased with us.
Father, I do remember your call.
It just happened to be the day I wanted to end it all.

"Did I extend a helping hand to you?"
Oh, yes Father You most certainly did!
It was through that neat little kid.

While I was sitting in the park, he said, "Sir please don't cry."
"Don't you know? It was for you, too, that Jesus died."
Mommy and Daddy said, "It's on Him you must rely."

I had to say Thank You "Little Guy."
He smiled and said, "No Problem, God is a Mighty Big Guy!"
"He owns all the earth and sky!"

James 5:19 (NIV)
My brothers if one of you should wander from the truth, and someone should bring him back, remember this: Whoever turns a sinner from his error of his way will save him from death and cover a multitude of sin.

Dear Parents

Parents, your children may act like they are not listening.
But, remember, be it good or bad,
your words and actions will be glistening!

For when we least expect,
we see our behavior through their reenactment.
You must understand the man in the poem
was bound for hell's torment!

But for a "little guy" who told the Jesus story
that you enthusiastically shared,
One more lost Soul has been spared.

This is to all the Christian Parents
who are doing what they should,
Thank You and God Bless You!

Proverbs 16:21 (NIV)
The wise in heart are called discerning, and pleasant words promote instruction.

Strong Ties

Ties that bind us
In love, from up above;
Ties that keep us
From hate, down below.
Ties that send us
Out to find those in need.
Ties that bind us
To the Supplier of all needs.
Ties that allow us
To heed His call;
Ties that connect us
To Jesus, the one who died for our sins!
Ties that bind us
To His Heavenly Father,
That makes us, too.
His sons and daughters.
Do you have strong ties
Like these?
If not, get on your knees.
Acceptance of Jesus as our Savior is the only way
we inherit ties that free.

Galatians 4:7 (NIV)
You are an heir of God through Jesus Christ.

Galatians 4:7
Wherefore thou art no more a servant, but a son; and if a son, then an heir of God through Christ.

Forgiveness

To ask forgiveness, what a message!

To be forgiven, what a blessing!

Straight from Heaven

And God above

Sending down

His Special Love.

Nothing else works

To remove the pain,

Not to mention

The guilt that made you go insane.

Blessed be . . .

Blessed be in Jesus Name.

Just forgiven!

Ephesians 4:32 (NIV)
And be ye kind one to another, tenderhearted, forgiving one another, even as God for Christ's sake hath forgiven you.

Power and Might

Power and might
Always are rather tight.
Hand and hand,
And together they're out of sight.

All power and might
Were sent with God's angels in flight
To change our world,
Giving us real insight.

Power and might, most of the time are used to duel,
Having left many looking and feeling much like a fool.
Needless to say they didn't look too cool.
Much better use, God had in mind,
for He uses power and might as His divine tool.

Leaving the spiritually blind looking their part, a fool!

GOD

2 Chronicles 20:6 (NIV)

O Lord, God of our father, are you not the God who is in Heaven? You rule over all the Kingdoms of the nations. Power and might are in your hand, and no one can withstand you.

God's Anointing

God's anointing upon our life
Is what protects us from harm and sustains through all strife.

Nothing can grasp hold when God is in control.
He is always there for us, protecting and comforting our soul.

Do not allow yourself to become spiritually blind,
Just trust in the Lord with all of your heart and mind.

God's awesome and mysterious ways
Always brightens even our darkest days.

Before you get out of bed to begin your day,
Don't forget to take time to pray.

For we never know what the day may hold,
But when God saves your soul, anointed you become,
and Satan loses all grasp of your immortal soul!

Psalm 105:15 (NIV)
Saying, touch not my anointed, and do my prophets no harm.

His Love Spreads Like English Ivy

Are you feeling hopeless and searching for ways to die?
God can hear even the faintest cry.

God can hear, heal, and take away all fear.
God will fill you with His Love, oh so Dear.

God's Love is much like "English Ivy." It spreads and takes over fast.
Ivy works through brick and mortar. God's Love works through pain and sorrow, direct results of sins in the past.

The beauty of the English Ivy never fades away,
and
The beauty of this story, is God's Love for us, is here to stay.

So if you are having a terrible day,
Remember, God hears the faintest cry and He is always there to help and lead the way.

Don't let your prayer time go till you get to this point.
God is always listening and just waiting to anoint.

Call on Him anytime,
Going down the road or waiting in line.

Remember, He is always there be it good times or bad.
Don't just wait until you're in a bind.
or you may be left behind.

1 John 4:19 (NIV)
We love, because He first loved us.

The Hollow of His Hand

God strategically created The Heavens and The Earth,
He measured the water in "The Hollow Of His Hand."

In His creation of water, the survival of all were in mind.
In life, seventy-percent is required for mankind.

He created The Heavens and The Earth in six, short days.
The seventh, He created The Sabbath for rest and study of His ways.

He formed man from the dust of ground, the Earth's surface.
God said man is not to be alone. He needs a helpmate in place.

God caused Adam to deeply sleep. He then took a rib from Adam.
Using a rib, a helpmate named Eve was formed by The Great I Am!

God's greatest creation was given dominion over all the Earth.
From the start to the end, there must be measured water for birth.

His Son's love was measured by outstretched arms.
He died for our sins, to be living water for our lost and thirsty souls . . .

Isaiah 40:12 (NIV)
Who hath measured the waters in the hollow of His hand, and meted out heaven with the span, and comprehended the dust of the earth in a measure, and weighed the mountains in scales, and the hills in a balance?

Ebb and Flow

The Ebb and Flow
Marks the tide as it comes and goes.

All in effort just to show
It is God's love that makes the waves roll.

Giving the empty Seashell
A never-ending story of love to tell.

Psalms 89:9
Thou rulest the raging of the sea: when the waves thereof arise, thou stillest them.

Rainbows and Smiles

God put the Rainbow in the Sky,
A beautiful sign to remind us on Him we must rely.

He knew in our lives there would be sad and gloomy days.
The Rainbow is just one of His special up-lifting displays.

He is always aware of our emotions, always concerned how we feel.
He knew the Rainbow in the Sky to our emotional side would appeal.

So don't you forget, when you see a Rainbow in the Sky,
The Smile on your face that automatically appears, is from God on high.

Even if your heart is sad, not yet Joy filled,
Isn't it amazing that a Smile spills instant Joy to a heart sorrow filled?

"Rainbows and Smiles" are some custom designs,
Specifically designed to Bless, giving Hope and Peace to our minds.

Many think no big deal!
The Revelation of truth must, be revealed!

It is no longer a secret. God designed "Rainbows and Smiles" to Heal!
My Dear Friend, that is a mighty BIG DEAL!

Genesis 9:15
And I will remember my covenant, which is between me and you and every living creature of all flesh; and the waters shall no more become a flood to destroy all flesh.

Our Creator

There is none greater
Than our Redeemer and Creator.

Satan tries to be His imitator.
But, he is just a manipulator.

His lies and tricks fill us with doubt.
It is in the name of Jesus we must shout.

Remove us from the deceitful Fantasy Land.
Show us the way to our Father's Promised Land,

So we can finally see our Navigator.
He is our Lord Jesus, The Son of God, Our Creator.

Exodus 18:11

Now I know that the Lord is greater than all gods: for in the thing wherein they dealt proudly He was above them.

Troubles Today

We all face troubles from day to day.
However, in God's Word we are reminded this too shall pass away.

Please accept expressions of God's love for the sorrow this brings.
In God's Word we all also are told, that there is a time for all things.

This will be for a brief moment only, just a detour in life's journey.
We shall thank God that the feelings of sorrow we feel right now
will not last for an eternity.

We shall not allow fear and doubt to creep in
because of these troubles seemingly undue.
For God's Holy Spirit is there for me and you,
Sent just to save, comfort, and carry us through.

Ecclesiastes 3:1
To every thing there is a season, and a time to every purpose under the heaven.

Infinite Wisdom

Father God, Your wisdom gives guidance for all generations
as was written so long ago.
T'was written for our world, dying in ignorance,
all lessons taught for our over-inflated ego.

Heavenly Father, we thank You for Your infinite wisdom,
for it will never be exceeded.
Father, please forgive our ignorance,
it has been Your messages we have not heeded!

It should be of no wonder of ours, why?
All of our endeavors have been shot down!
It is Your wisdom that is most profound.

Thank You, Father, for placing us on solid ground.
It is through Your love and infinite wisdom
we are now Heaven bound!

You bore our stripes and carried our shame.
I hate to mention Your suffering of deep pain.

Through these horrific events, our lives are forever changed!
Now it is time for a priority change.
Life is much easier when God has rearranged.

Job 5:27

Lo this, we have searched it, so it is, hear it, and know thou it for thy good.

God's Communication

Modern technology, computers, and the web's race,
Can't ever compare to God's infinite wisdom and pace.

No matter the intellect,
With His infinite wisdom, it is you that He'll not neglect.

His divine communication is individual, and is based on our level,
Unlike any other genuinely unique,
and very much unlike that of the devil!

The Holy Spirit allows the deaf to hear His loving voice,
The blind to see His plans with great choice.
Even the paralyzed can feel His presence,
God allows all of us the choice to give Him residence.

Man cannot create equipment to communicate with God.
The most sophisticated tool, the Holy Spirit,
God's design for direct communication with God.

It is by faith and through prayer
we are allowed to communicate realistically.
God hears and answers our prayers
no matter the depth, even when given simplistically.

Jeremiah 33:3

Call unto me, and I will shew thee great my mighty things which thou knowest not.

Unmerited Favor

It was unmerited favor given by our Dear Savior.

—Thank You Father God.—

My life was filled with unacceptable behavior.

—Father it saddens me to know, my sinful choices were something that you could see—

Many things that happened
were kept only between you and me.
—For all my choices in this life now I pray
be fully acceptable unto Thee.—

Deep sorrow filled my heart from insight given. I was not the child you planned me to be.

—Dear Father, forgive me.—

The horrible thought of you innocently crucified
for sinners such as me.
That is "Unmerited Favor," and it bought this awful sinner
to bended knee.

—Thank You, Father God, it's your forgiving Grace Unmerited that set me free.—

Ephesians 1:7 (NIV)
In Him we have redemption through His blood, the forgiveness of sins, in accordance with the riches of God's grace that he lavished on us with all wisdom and understanding.

Human's Race

Discovering God's Grace
Should be the race above all races.
No other race could take its place.
Life has too much to bear
If with the Father you don't share
All your burdens and cares.
It's for you the road He's prepared.
Go to the Father in prayer,
Just ask Him to lift your load,
And keep you on that straight and narrow road.
Remember, when you can't keep the pace,
It's with the Father you need to go face to face.

1 Peter 1:13

Wherefore gird up the loins of your mind, be sober, and hope to the end for the grace that is to be bought unto you at the revelation of Jesus Christ.

From Your Grace I Fell

From Your grace I fell,
I was headed straight to hell;
The Holy Spirit breathed on me,
Revealing God's love to me
For all the world to see,
From sinful addictions,
Bodily affliction,
And Satan's contradictions.
He will do the same for you
What He's done for me.
He will set you free,
Condemned, unclean,
You'll no longer be.
No longer to live in fear,
Knowing God is always near;
It is He that you should fear,
For it is you and I He holds dear.

Job 1:8 (NIV)
Then the Lord said to Satan, "Have you considered my servant Job? There is no one on earth like him; he is blameless and upright, a man who fears God and shuns evil."

GUIDANCE

Harsh Words

Harsh words cut like a knife,
always causing us the most grief in life.
Cutting deep to the bone,
Nothing can remove the memory of that harsh tone.

It keeps playing over and over in our mind.
How can one say words that are so unkind?
The person whom you love the most,
Has just been the unkind host.

The reminding host of a ghost from a sinful past;
It's a haunt that lasts; so very hard, for all
to let go of the past,
Forgiven and forgotten by God and His Son only.
God takes away the pain and fear
that makes you feel sad and lonely.

To remove the pain and sorrow on our own,
would be a ridiculous endeavor.
For we are not capable, and the memories linger forever.
But God gives us guidance to guide us in whatever the endeavor.
Under all circumstances harsh words should not be used, NOT EVER!

Proverbs 15:1 (NIV)
A gentle answer turns away wrath, but a harsh stirs up anger.

Wake Up

There is no time to spare in the believer's life.
God told us to make use of our time, telling all how to rid their strife.

We are to be accountable unto Him for every single minute.
In knowing Christ, His love compels us to help the less fortunate.

Look around—Can't you see pain and suffering as the broken cry?
That is exactly why there is no time for me, myself and I.

The broken need a Savior they, too, can call unto,
But without you, they will not know whom to turn to.

The broken spend their spare time in total despair.
All are in need of "The Holy Spirit" to set them free, only Christ can spare.

Don't continue to waste your time, leaving the lost no sight of Grace.
Take the opportunity to share the knowledge of God's Amazing Grace.

How else will they get to meet "The Savior" face to face?

Romans 13:11,13 (NAS)
Do this, knowing the time, that it is already the hour for you to awaken from sleep; for now salvation is nearer to us than when we believed. Let us behave properly as in the day, not in carousing and drunkenness, not in sexual promiscuity and sensuality, not in strife and jealousy.

Unstable Ground

Thank you, Father, for carrying me while on unstable ground.
As I look back through time,
Your footprints reassure me You were around.

Thank you for Your loving arms that always surround,
Carrying me beyond my struggles
before ever letting me stand ground.

Leaving the cross I was trying to bear in shifting sand.
Thanks to You, Father, I am a little closer to the Promised Land.

While on life's journey traveling upon unsteady ground,
You carried me to serenity, a place no other way could ever be found.

The only way to survive life's stairway of shifting sand
Is by holding on to Your Saving hand.

Because when You feel us slip, before we ever fall,
We find ourselves in Your arms, before we even had time to call.

Isaiah 40:11
He shall feed his flock like a Shepherd: he shall gather the lambs with his arm, and carry them in his bosom, and shall gently lead those that are with young.

Out of His Will

Living out of God's Will, there is no peace or joy.
You're doomed to die when you become Satan's toy.

God's Son, Jesus Christ, will give you everlasting joy.
Satan fills you with depression in hopes to destroy.

Removing the blinds in repentance of only the world's view
Allows growth in the knowledge of Christ to begin in you.

With the true knowledge of Christ comes wisdom
And
Victory over Satan's planned destruction of spiritual freedom.

It is God's Will, that you seek Him with all of your heart.
Then, Dear One, in Christ you are doing your part.

This is how we allow God to Bless us every step of the way.
We are to pass this message on to all we meet each day.

For it is in God's Word we must daily stay.
Otherwise, Satan will take hold allowing our mission to sway.

Romans 12:2
And be not conformed to this world: but be ye transformed by the renewing of your mind, that ye may prove what is good, and acceptable, and perfect, will of God.

Stand by Father

Life from you has already been given.
It is just my sinful living
And my heart to you that has yet to be given.

I've been told I must give up the sinful way of life I've been living
So a life with meaning I can start sowing.
In return, I will start by giving back to you.

I must seek the lost and tell them about you.
How through your Grace and by your Love they too can have life anew.
Thanks for the mission. I'll be following through.

Please Stand by, Father, for I will be calling more and more upon you,
For it is in all areas of my life, I now solely depend on you.
Thank you for your guidance; I will be doing what you need me to do.

It is in Your Precious Name, Jesus,
I pray to follow You.

Proverbs 24:6 (NIV)
For the waging of war you need guidance, and victory many advisers.

Don't Grumble

When I hear people grumble and complain,
Nobody needs to explain.

They're missing the point,
It is the willing whom God chooses to anoint.

Not those who sit around and compare.
It is His Word that He wants us to talk about and share.

But if they insist and continue to compare,
Tell them it is their life to Jesus, if they dare?

Since they dare not, let them compare not.
And let us spare not, one of those grumbling people,
Who care not!

They have not met our Savior,
Or He would have changed their behavior.

James 5:9 (NIV)
Don't grumble against each other, brothers, or you will be judged.
The Judge is standing at the door.

Your Kingdom
The Ultimate Freedom

Heaven

No more Sickness . . .

No more Pain . . .

No more doubt . . .

No more Fear . . .

Down here on Earth,
Cause that's JESUS
And His Angels,
I See . . .

He is my Eternal Father and He is coming
For me . . .
Oh Glory Be!
It's Heaven I see!

Psalms 16:11
Thou wilt shew me the path of life: In thy presence is fullness of joy; At thy right hand is pleasure for evermore.

Listen

You must choose to listen and accept the Holy Spirit.

Satan will always be in your face.
Testing and trying you, he wants to leave you in disgrace.

Remember, Satan has no real connection,
he enters only through lies and deception.

Without the Holy Spirit in your possession,
You are stuck without any power to stand against Satan
in rejection.

Obedience to & possession of the Holy Spirit gives you strength
to withstand all forces.
Listening to the Holy Spirit is not like listening
to deceitful voices.

For when the Holy Spirit speaks, along comes great strength,
Unlike the fear that Satan delivers,
making one feel as if they are going to sink.
Thank you Father for your power can save us from harm in a blink.

1 John 4:4
Greater is he who is in me than he that is in the world.

Chances Are

When everything seems to be going wrong,
Chances are that's true.
Maybe you are stuck without even the slightest clue,
Just what it is, you're supposed to do.

Have you posed the question to yourself,
I wonder what God wants me to do?
Then it should be of no surprise to you
Why the Holy Spirit has not revealed God's plan
as to what you're to do.
Pose the question in acknowledgment to Him.
He will reveal exactly what to do!

Proverbs 3:6

In all thy ways acknowledge him and he will direct thy paths.

A Steady Flow

The Holy Spirit is in a steady flow,
And always yields understanding, strength and love within the flow.

We sometimes lose awareness of His special anointing,
Somehow forgetting that God does all the appointing.

Getting too wrapped up in our own personal ability
Leads us down the dead-end road with all signs pointing
to our inability.

Reliance on God for our every need,
Is the message He has given and He trusted we would heed?

For failing to realize He is in control,
He brings us to humility, yielding His strength with love in a steady flow.

His gift of The Holy Spirit comes with no broken leads.
With His infinite wisdom, He gave the only gift that could
supply all of our needs.

That is why He made each of us with a vital need for He.
Always knowing never to solely rely on the help from anyone except Thee.

Romans 8:31
What shall we say to these things? If God be for us, who can be against us?

Fruit of the Spirit

Forbidden fruit still abound.

But, it's Your Love
That keeps me spiritually bound.

In reading Your Word,

It's Your guidance

That I seek.

While on my knees

It's for Your Will,

Your Way,
and for The
Fruit of Your Spirit,

Dear Lord,
That
I continuously pray.

Ephesians 5:9
(For the fruit of the Spirit is in all goodness and righteousness and truth:)

Peaceful Place

We must not allow Satan's injected evil thoughts,
to occupy our mind.
His thoughts are always evil,
the most destructive kind.

There is only one way to keep evil,
from occupying any mental space.
Is to tell Satan, he doesn't belong in this place!

In the name of Jesus command Satan to leave!
He will flee without a trace!
The Holy Spirit will erase all evil
in the name of Jesus in any case,

When we allow The Holy Spirit to occupy our inner space.
Because of our trust in Thee, The Holy Spirit makes our mind
a peaceful place.

Isaiah 26:3

Thou wilt keep him in perfect peace, whose mind is stayed on Thee: Because he trusteth in Thee.

Anticipation

I can't wait without great anticipation,
Awe to reach the realm of glory where Angels sing
with great inspiration.
Our Heavenly Father is the great inspirer.
To be like Him is my greatest desire.

Father, show me Thy great and mighty way.
Ever increasing is the anticipation with each passing day.

Please keep me on your path in the midst of worldly craze,
A craze that keeps lost sheep in a constant daze.

As I journey on Your extended mission,
Please help me to see with Your Holy Vision.

My continuous prayer to You, Heavenly Father,
Send The Holy Spirit before me, with me and behind me
so I am not a bother.
Prepare their hearts, minds and souls.
Please give me strength to accomplish Your given goals.

For all who do not know,
It is The Holy Spirit that ministers to lost souls!

Luke 12:12

For the Holy Spirit shall teach you at that time what you should say.

Discernment

Oh Father, glorious is Your Love and Grace.
We must share Your Inspiring Word for the lost world to taste.

No other written text is so loving or complex.
The stories that fill The Holy Bible to most, will certainly perplex.

It takes The Holy Spirit to discern what is within.
The only way to have this discernment is to invite God's Son, Jesus, in.

He enters your heart to cleanse and free
from all past sin and worldly trash.
For the trash within the sinful man and The Holy Spirit will clash!

Now freed by God's Son, you become in tune with, "The Mind of Christ."
When tempted by evil, with such discernment, you won't think twice.

The Holy Spirit speaks loud and clear,
Giving His Children such boldness, that it relinquishes all fear,

Letting you constantly know that your Heavenly Father holds you Dear.
He will never leave or forsake you. In His Word, He made that clear.

1 Kings 3:9
Give therefore they servant an understanding heart to judge thy people, that I may discern between good and bad:

Hebrews 13:5
Let your conversation be without covetousness; and be content with such things as you have: for he hath said, I will never leave thee, nor forsake thee.

Meet Jesus First

It is Jesus you must first meet.
Then, it is His Will, you must seek.

Some people may even think you're a freak
Until at Jesus they, too, take a peak.

None of us have a clue
Just what it is we're supposed to do.

In fact, most of us improvise
Until, the Holy Spirit gives us a life completely revised.

Oh, what a surprise!
We no longer have the need to improvise

With the Holy Spirit within, we now realize.
It is our future, we no longer let sin jeopardize!

Psalms 143:10
Teach me to do thy will; for thou art my God: thy spirit is good; lead me into the land of uprightness.

Renewing of the Mind

There is no humanly way possible to do it.
Only God, through The Holy Spirit, can renew it.

But He won't do it without us. That means you, too.
He gives us two choices, one of which we must choose.

Keep in mind, on one hand, we have absolutely nothing to lose.
On the other hand, we have everything to lose.

With temptation all around, Satan is in hopes we will mess up.
The battle is won when we drink from the surrender prayer cup.

Renewing of the mind is at its best
When to Jesus we surrender and our sins we confess,

Allowing The Holy Spirit to enter, renewing our mind.
Let us give praise unto Him! We have left the old man behind.

Ephesians 4:23-24
And be renewed in the spirit of your mind; and that ye put on the new man, which after God is created in righteousness and true holiness.

My Darkest Hour

In my
Darkest hour
Was when God sent His power!

The only power that could deliver
The pain and misery that Satan had delivered!

When "The Holy Spirit" appeared,
Old Satan's evil spirit suddenly disappeared!

Feeling "The Holy Spirit" flow through me
Is the most awesome feeling that could ever be!

My darkest hour, Oh, how I can still remember,
But, I went to God and He took away my sins never to be remembered!

Thank You, Father, in Jesus Precious Name!

1 John 3:24 (NIV)
Those who obey His commands live in Him, and He in them. And this we know that He lives in us: We know it by the spirit He gave us.

I Am Protected

Get out of my way Satan!
It is not your sinful ways I am contemplating.

It is a method in which to reach the weak,
Before you sneak in and make them think
their life looks dreadfully bleak!

You better run, Satan for there has been a leak.
"The Holy Spirit" is flowing and it is you "The Spirit" seeks.

You don't understand,
It is "The True Solid Rock" on which I stand.

This means: I am protected by "The Blood of the Lamb."
Therefore, I through "The Holy Spirit"
recognize you and your foolish scams!

Psalm 18:2

The Lord is my rock, and my fortress and my deliverer, my God, my strength, in whom I will trust; My buckler and the horn of my salvation, and my high tower.

Our Role

Hope

As Christians we need to play our role.
That means we need to let God be in control.

To be more specific, that means our thoughts and actions, too,
In every single thing we do.

We can't allow Satan to have any control.
So, you better get in touch with whom you've been told.

Jesus Christ,
He is
The only One
Who
Truly has control.
You must allow Him to lead
You
For the fulfillment of your
Role.

Hebrews 13:8 (NIV)
Jesus Christ is the same yesterday and today and forever.

Shelter Me, Father

Shelter me Father, when the storms of life come.
Shelter me Father, I pray Thy will be done.

Shelter me Father, old Satan is on the prowl.
Shelter me Father, from my thoughts of throwing in the towel.

Shelter me Father, from the fear of being alone.
Shelter me Father, by reminding me, You are still on the Throne.

Shelter me Father, for I am weak and Ye are strong.
Shelter me Father, keeping me from all that's wrong.

Shelter me Father, being with you, is my heart's desire.
Shelter me Father, until it is from this earth, I retire.

Then Dear Father I'll be singing praises unto you, in Heaven's Choir
It is there I'll be wearing a white robe for my new attire.

Psalm 61:3
For thou has been a shelter for me, and a strong tower from the enemy.

Pity

I was feeling kind of down,
Until I looked around;
All I could see was your beauty looking back at me.
You gave me life not only for here, but for throughout eternity.

Father, please forgive me for being so selfish.
I was being a bit childish,
I know you understand,
Thank you for giving me your lifting hand.

I am no longer playing in "Pity's Band."

Matthew 22:29

Jesus answered and said unto them, ye do err, not knowing the Scriptures, nor the Power of God.

Grace Filled

Through the pain and suffering, gracefully we endured,
God makes it worth our while, this we are assured.

Departing this life here on earth
Gracefully relieves feelings of hurt.

So, for the remainder of time we have here on loan,
We can gracefully prepare for our Heavenly home.

We will gracefully be waiting for our Father's call.
Gracefully speaking, that is the most important call of all.

We would not want to deprive anyone of their Heavenly home.
We need not let them aimlessly continue to roam.

It was for all, His Son on the cross, painfully did moan.
He, for Grace, suffered and died. He knew He was never alone.

He knew God, The Father, was sadly viewing from The Throne.
He didn't pass the cup of pain and suffering, and now He's home.

Truly blessed are we, for He is with God The Father hand in hand
Way yonder in the Promised Land.

Romans 5:2
By whom also we have access by faith into this grace wherein we stand, and rejoice in hope of the glory of God.

Domestic Violence

So often kept in silence,
For the very fact that most people can't conceive it,
While many others choose not to see or believe it.
The strain, the pain, they are all so hard to explain.
Our feelings must remain refrained,
Always searching for the right words to use,
Avoiding at all cost the abuse.
The silent cries meet the eyes of many who have survived it.
There is Hope! There is Help!
It is to God, that you must cry out;
He will show you the way out, no doubt.
You must allow Him to help you to sever the binding chain.
Or else,
You take the sure risk of death or going mentally insane. . . .
Just call upon His Name.
You will never be the same!

Isaiah 57:21
There is no peace, saith my God, to the wicked.

Simplicity

Life was meant to be simple
Without many cares!

We must beware, for Satan at our simplicity tears.
After his tugs and snare, his gift to you is ten million cares.
God's gift is the Holy Spirit
sent to relieve us from all of our despair;
God's greatest design is The Holy Spirit
it was sent to give us Joy, with enough to share.

When temptation is delivered,
Through the Holy Spirit, we will know in an instant
that it is Satan who dares.
Once we have gained knowledge of the Truth,
we must never forget,
It is our Lord Jesus, who sent us the greatest gift.

1 John 3:5
And ye know that He was manifested to take away our sin; and in Him is no sin.

Our Savior's Love

Great is the Love of our Dear Savior.
He loves us unconditionally, that means regardless of our childish behavior,

He will deliver us from our selfish ways,
Giving us something to talk about, allowing us to give to Him continuous praise.

So don't forget, Our Heavenly Father tells us to ask.
Come on, you know, that's no major task!

Living with the burden is much harder to do,
Than going to our knees and giving it up to we know whom?

So the next time we're wondering what to do,
We must go to our Heavenly Father. He will be sending His immediate blessings out to us.

We may not receive the answer we would expect.
However, many times our will and His are different,
With His infinite wisdom we must willfully accept.

We will better understand,
When in Heaven we shall stand.
For at the reading,

All revealing will take place, when in Heaven we stand,
By the grand event of the unrolling scroll of
God's Master plan!

Proverbs 11:11

By the blessing of the upright the city is exalted: but it is overthrown by the mouth of the wicked.

Master Savior

Master, Savior, it's like you we long to be,
For You are blameless and sin-free.

To comprehend that You died on the cross for sinners, such as we,
It is not easy for us to comprehend, just how that could ever be.

It is certainly clear to all that Your Love, Kindness, and Mercy
Astonishes those of us, who take the time to see.

Father, Thank You, for setting us free from the bondage of our sin,
For now, we can clearly see that the awesome Love that abides
within, is Definitely from Thee.

John 8:36 (NIV)
So if the Son sets you free, you are free indeed.

God's Son

Jesus had a major job to get done
Just because He's God's Son . . .

No race or creed could slow His speed
Just because He's God's Son . . .

He sincerely cared about everyone
Just because He's God's Son . . .

Jesus suffered and died on the cross, to save the lost
Just because He's God's Son . . .

He healed the sick, be they lame or blind
Just because He's God's Son . . .

He turned the water into wine
Just because He's God's Son . . .

He calmed the raging storm
Just because He's God's Son . . .

He warned Noah about the Flood
Just because He's God's Son . . .

From His birth to resurrection, He sent people in the right direction
Just because He's God's Son . . .

He loves us unconditionally, for instance the woman at the well . . .

What a mission, a mission well done . . .
All because of love between "The Father" and "The Son."

John 3:16
For God so loved the world, that he gave his only begotten Son, that whosoever believeth in him should not perish, but have ever lasting life.

Hebrews 4:14
Seeing then that we have a great high priest, that is passed into the heavens, Jesus the Son of God, let us hold fast our profession.

The Amazing Story

We all ask the question, where do we fit in?
Let me tell you, my friend . . .

Putting Jesus first in your life is where you begin.
Repentance is a must for we all struggle everyday with sin.

If you're not fulfilling your God-called mission,
You will never know what spiritual blessings you are missing.

Don't stop giving of yourself.
Jesus never stopped giving of Himself.

Now you know the full story,
And to Him be all the Glory.

When your mission is complete . . . you'll be in Glory!
Now, my friend, that is an Amazing Story . . .

John 15:9

As the Father hath loved me, so have I loved you: continue in my love.

Jesus Is Willing

Jesus is willing.
What about you?

Jesus loves you.
What about you?

Jesus fulfilled His call.
What about you?

Jesus keeps His word.
What about you?

Jesus loves His children unconditionally.
What about you?

Jesus obeyed His Father.
What about you?

Jesus walked the Straight and Narrow.
What about you?

Jesus died to self.
What about you?

Psalms 32:8
I will instruct thee and teach thee in thy way which thou shalt go;
I will guide thee with mine eye.

Jesus Heard the Call

Jesus took call for the entire human race;
Thank You Father for taking my place.
Had it not been for Your Abundant Love and Amazing Grace,
I would never get to see You, face to face.

While I am here on Earth, with all of my heart
I will seek out Your will and work hard to do my part.
You took my place on the cross for all the sins that I committed.
For this, dear sweet Savior, to You I'll always be submitted.

My troubles and trials I once faced alone.
Now because of You, sweet Savior, I'll never be alone.
Dear Jesus, with You on the throne,
God, our Father in Heaven, is not alone.

Until Your return, I must be here,
Always knowing You're near,
Holding my hand; thus removing all fear.
I'm waiting patiently, Father, until You appear.

Revelation 21:2–6a (NAS)

And I saw the holy city, new Jerusalem, coming down out of heaven from God, made ready as a bride adorned for her husband. And I heard a loud voice from the throne, saying, "Behold, the tabernacle of God is among men, and He shall dwell among them, and they shall be His people, and God Himself shall be among them, and He shall wipe away every tear from their eyes; and there shall no longer be any death; there shall no longer be any mourning, or crying or pain; the first things have passed away." And He said, "Write, for these words are faithful and true." And He said to me, "It is done, I am the Alpha and the Omega, the beginning and the end."

No Explanation

No individual can quite explain
Why Jesus did not escape the pain.

He was only doing exactly what His Father ordained.

God had sent Him, and He was His only Son.
God alone knew that there was much work that must be done.

Along the way Jesus planted many a seed,
Healing the sick, helping all He came in contact with,
supplying them with their greatest need.

Telling them to repent of their sins,
for salvation alone was their greatest need, indeed.
Jesus knew His mission was to help all of us succeed.

First, we have to allow Him to remove from our hearts hate and greed.
Fueling us with love and the serviceability,
to perform kind deeds to those who are in need.

2 Peter 1:9 (NAS)
For He who lacks these qualities is blind or short sighted, having forgotten his purification from his former sins.

Judgement

Living in judgment by others of our actions while here on earth
Is not comparable to the judgment of our actions
when we depart from earth.

Facing the Father should be our only fear.
While on earth our judgment by others is merely for here.

Judgment in Heaven is of all sins we did not ask to be forgiven.
So while on earth we are held accountable
for the way we are living.
In reading His word we choose our actions
by following His commands,
It sure makes judgment in Heaven
much easier to understand.

Meanwhile, I am trying to prepare before the Father I stand.
Please, reach down Dear Savior and hold my hand.

Deuteronomy 32:39–41 (NIV)

See now that I myself am He! There is no God besides me. I put to death and bring to life, I wounded and I will heal, No one can deliver from my hand. I lift my hand to Heaven and declare: As surely as I live forever, when I sharpen my flashing sword and my hand grasps it in judgment I will take vengeance on my adversaries and repay those who hate me.

Cast a Stone

Is that a stone I see?
You best get out
From in front of me,
For if it is my sin
Only
That you see,

There is much trouble
Up ahead for you.
But it won't be from me.
It will be from Thee.

Don't let me stand in your way
On this one-way path;
Because it is The Savior
That you must make haste to meet.

He traveled this road,
The only one without any sin.
He said, "We would all fall short,
No one can do it but He."

He said, "To anyone without any sin
You may cast the first stone.
So, You best drop your stone,
It is definitely time for you to be on your way, be gone!"

'John 8:7b

He that is without sin among you, let him cast a stone at her.

Anoint My Words

I dare not share with just anyone my troubles today.
I dare not, for it may knock them down or cause them to sway.

I chose to share with God only when I pray,
Thus allowing Him to anoint my words in all I say.

My casual conversation must be about God's Saving Grace.
It is only by His Grace that we are able to keep up the pace.

Our world is filled with negativity at every level in all places,
Just look around. It is painted across the world
on our faces.

To dig into the lives of most, on a shallow level,
Would reflect the terrible works of destruction left
by the devil.

We must work eagerly to spread the Good News,
Letting all know they have the right to choose.

Whom they will follow and allow to rein as the God of their life,
Thus removing all grief before inevitably causing much strife.

Father, I want to Thank You for becoming the God of my life.
I was not able to continue in the midst of continuous strife.

Proverbs 10:12
Hatred stirreth up strifes: but love covereth all sins.

Escape Being Defiled

The only way to escape all that is within
Is to ask our Dear Savior to come in.

—Filling us with His Wonderful Love—

It is what we have within that defiles us.
Seeking God and His will is all that delivers us.

—Rise up from all foolishness.—

"Evil thoughts, adultery, fornication, murder,
stealing, covetousness, wickedness,
Lasciviousness, evil eyes, blasphemy, pride, foolishness and deceit"
Only God can make you complete.

Let us lend an ear to hear God's message.
It is one of the many ways He intended to bless us.

Mark 7:20

And He said, that which cometh out of the man, that defileth the man.

Tulips

The Tulips glisten as the Sun gently kisses them,
Realizing both the Tulips and the Sun are beautiful gifts from Him.

To see them moving, in the gentle breeze
Reminds me how the Father, from sin and pain, He gently frees.

Enjoy the gentle reminder as you behold such beauty.
Always remember, such beauty only comes from Thee.

Oh, great is the Joy in knowing He made them just for you and me,
For He knew the pleasure they would bring for us to see.

Father, Thank You for allowing this opportunity.
I know in season the flowers with color will fade,
But there is Great Joy in knowing, Your Love and Words will never fade away . . .

1 Peter 1:24–25

For all flesh is as grass, and all the glory of man as the flower of grass. The grass withereth, and the flower thereof falleth away: But the word of the Lord endureth for ever. And this is the word which by the gospel is preached unto you.

Margins of Society Widen

The margins of a bizarre society are widening.
To be quite honest with you, it's frightening.

Open your eyes and see all the lost people in need of Jesus Christ.
They are looking to see if there are any people around
who are sincerely nice?

When you see someone in need,
Do you stop and offer assistance so in life they, too, can succeed?

Don't avoid those who you know are in need.
God's message must have gone in one ear and out the other,
for it you do not heed.

It sounds like it's time to kneel in prayer.
It is for all, Our Lord Jesus, wants us to extend care.

You better find your Bible and take time to read.
If understanding isn't easy, pray for wisdom and allow God to lead.

You will be amazed what God will reveal to you.
Your prayers will be answered, the lost will be saved
and God will bless you, in all you do.

It is then that the margins of society will widen in Christ,
Creating a better world. Now, you can see, we don't have time to think twice.

We are called to go out into the world.

John 3:16

For God so loved the world, he gave his only begotten Son, that whosoever believeth in him, should not perish, but have everlasting life.

Not a Choice—A Command

Love is an emotion that can be expressed in many different ways.
The different expressions in our mind forever stays.

We learn throughout our lives many uncompromising ways to be kind.
But to the diverse, God constantly has to remind.

Diverse are those who differ from what we consider to be the norm.
Conveniently being preoccupied, its diversity we choose to ignore.

Never realizing by ignoring diversity we allow God's truth to be stored.
That's not what God had in mind when He sent His Son
whom He adored.

God sent His Son, Jesus, for all mankind.
Why do we choose indifference? For it's a loving God
that draws the line.

John 13:34 (NIV)
A new command I give you: Love one another. As I have loved you, so you must love one another. All men will know that you are my disciples if you love one another.

Strength to Endure

Think not of the sins that flooded your past.
But, Thank God. He has forgiven you; all you had to do was ask.

Focus on the things that are good and pure,
For it is God's Love that gives us the strength to endure.

The words and actions of others may take you by surprise,
But you must always turn to The Father for His Love never dies.

He will take away hurt by giving a double portion of His Love.
Don't forget to Thank Him for the outpour from above.

So when you're faced with harsh words from those you love,
Don't go searching for your verbal punching glove.

Just take them to The Father in prayer.
He will shed the pain they just freely gave you to bear.

They, too, will receive a blessing from Heaven, and the world will
be a better place because for them, you earnestly prayed.

1 Chronicles 16:34 (NIV)
Give thanks to the Lord, for he is good; his love endures forever.

Your Love Prevailed

Your Amazing Grace is such an awesome gift.
It was my soul that you did lift.

I was living near the pits of hell,
And that within itself, was an emotional jail.

The Holy Spirit fell on me, that is when "Your Love prevailed!"

To live with Your Love and Hope,
Gives new meaning to life, for now I can cope.

Though once sad and constantly depressed,
Because, my life was full of sins that I had never taken the time to confess!

Father God, Thank You for Your Holy Spirit,
There is no power in this life that can come near it!

For a sinner such as I, they must be told there is a way out of despair,
It's Your Love that doth prevail and there is nothing that can compare.

1 Samuel 2:9
He will keep the feet of his saints, and the wicked shall be silent in darkness; for by strength shall no man prevail.

Every Sinner's Dream

My heart almost skips a beat,
It's just the thought of sitting at your feet.

Though not worthy, it was your Grace,
I got to meet.

My sin sick soul You cleansed so clean,
That is every sinner's dream.

You came to me and pierced my heart,
You gave me a new start.

You filled my heart with your unconditional love,
You are My Dear Savior from Heaven above.

Philippians 1:9
And this I pray, that your love may abound yet more and more in knowledge and in all judgment.

Submissive Woman

Mission

God is sending me on a mission,
Calling the broken hearted woman into submission.

However, it is not upon the demands of an earthly man

To a loving Heavenly Father,
So they too, can be called His daughter.

He loves you unconditionally.

Yes, Oh yes, Satan wants to remind you
Where you've been, and what you have done.

You can receive FORGIVENESS through the Father's Son.

None of us are worthy.
We all fall short.

That is the beauty of His story.

It's MERCY, MERCY, MERCY,
Filled with unconditional Love and Amazing Grace
And to GOD be all the GLORY!

Deuteronomy 31:6

Be strong and of good courage: fear not nor be afraid of them: for the Lord thy God, he it is that doth go with thee; he will not fail thee, nor forsake thee.

God Made You Unique

Don't try your mission alone, read God's word.
Going solo in times of old or present have proven to be absurd.

Don't forget about God until you become an antique.
No one can do your job. God made you special! That makes you unique.

Greet your neighbors, call a friend to make amends, be kind to all.
In a dark world, let your light shine, never forgetting your call.

There is no time for keeping up with The Jones's and all their doing.
It's the hypocritical behavior that you are to be subduing.

How could you forget that your reward is in Heaven? So work earnestly.
Don't play around by shirking your responsibility, work honestly.

2 Timothy 2:14–15 (NAS)
Remind them of these things, and solemnly charge them in the presence of God not to wrangle about words, which is useless, and leads to the ruin of the hearers. Be diligent to present yourself approved to God as a workman who does not need to be ashamed, handling accurately the word of truth.

A Hug a Day

A hug a day keeps anger away.
A hug a day radiates warmth and affection
an effort to share God's love each day.

A hug a day nurtures and leads a friend who has gone astray.
A hug a day is a simple act that extends God's Love
in a very special way.

A hug a day rapidly dries the tears of sadness entirely away.
A hug a day energizes the inner self to no longer stay
in a state of dismay.

A hug a day is the way to express a feeling that cannot be told.
A hug a day is for the young and the old.

A hug a day is for all!
It doesn't matter if you're big or small.

This is for the young and old, useful information, gained knowledge
that must be told!
A hug a day is as precious as gold . . .

Thank You, Father, for your loving embrace.
I am no longer just occupying space,
All because of your loving embrace.

Psalm 57:10 (NIV)
For great is your love, reaching to the heavens; your faithfulness reaches to the skies.

How

We let life get so busy,
We even take life for granted.

We must not forget,
There are seeds of salvation that need to be planted!

It is our job to make sure the seeds get planted
By letting the Holy Spirit plow the way.

Let us be Thankful and always remember to give Thanks
For Our Heavenly Father sends The Holy Spirit
to fill our soul's empty tank!

Let us not take for granted even a single day,
For it is in Jesus name we pray,
Amen

1 John 3:9 (NIV)
No one who is born of God will continue to sin, because God's seed remains in him; he cannot go on sinning, because he has been born of God.

Your Mission

There is no time for doubt,
You must tell Satan to get out.

No time left for despair,
There are people who need to know, somebody who gives a care!

God will speak to those who will listen.
For those who choose not,
no telling when they will come into submission.

Waiting on them, would be wasting salvation time.
There are millions of people who are standing in Hell's line.

They must be told to seek remission of their sins.
Telling them, through Jesus, spiritual life never ends.

It begins with forgiveness and continues throughout eternity.
What a Love-filled opportunity.

God sends out the call,
He even sent His Son Jesus to die for us all.

Luke 18:11
For the Son of man is come to save that which was lost.

Let Your Light Shine

We need not be rich by worldly standards.
We need only be rich in God's standards.

We must let our little light shine in a mighty way.
It is not the big things only that brighten our day.

It is the small and steady things that are sent from God above.
He sends them in His own personal way, in His pure love.

Creating smiles that brighten His Children's face.
Love in the form of a hug, so that we can feel His embrace.

That is truly Amazing Grace!

Matthew 5:16
Let your light shine before men, that they may see your good works, and glorify your Father which is in Heaven.

God's Candid View

If you don't like being in zoom's view,
Maybe because you are not doing what God wants you to do.

Are you living according to God's will?
If not, that may have something to do with the depression you feel.

Are you always feeling tired and continuously getting mad?
It's hard to get in the picture when you're wearing a frown and feeling sad.

How long has it been since you gave your face a lift?
Sounds like it's time for a little spiritual gift.

What must you do for such a gift?
Ask the Father in Jesus Name for help. He will redeem you just that swift.

That, for sure, will give your face a lift,
Giving you unspeakable Joy, What a Gift!

The Father with His candid view will definitely be watching over you!

I am praying for the depression, fear, and doubt
to be immediately removed from you!

John 16:24
Hitherto have ye asked nothing in my name: ask, and ye shall receive, that your joy may be full.

Obey

Consumed By Self's Desire

Our personal desires must be consumed in the fire.
It is God's way of removing our own personal desire.

God works continuously to bring us to our knees.
Our personal trials bring humility and it is through humility God frees.

Then advancement through spiritual growth occurs.
Obedience to The Lord's Will then spurs.

Our spiritual growth allows God to use us tirelessly,
No more defeated by personal desires foolishly.

We are now victorious Saints, by The Will of The Father.
We discovered God does not need our thoughts or desires, they are just our soul's bother.

During this time of being lonely and misunderstood,
I give Thanks unto God, otherwise understanding I never would.

Father, Thank You for this revelation on desires.
Forever realizing seeking Your Will is what our life requires.

1 John 5:14

And this is the confidence that we have in him, that if we ask anything according to his will, he heareth us:

Compassion

Compassion grows when we allow God to help us overcome self.
We will no longer put our neighbors needs on a shelf.

We will no longer be blinded by the temptation all about
Until we, by the authority of Christ, give Satan a shove out.

Our lives are yoked by self-centeredness accompanied with strife.
God must heal to remove strife, healing adds much peace to life.

This makes the world to those around us a delight.
You are one more Christian shoving Satan out of his spite.

Lamentations 3:22
It is of the Lord's mercies that we are not consumed, because his compassions fail not.

Willingness

Jesus spoke very clear, "He said your life is no joke!"
"You are on your way to hell."
It was on the cross that I posted your bail.

For years, I have been trying to get through to you.
I finally got your attention, now it's up to you. What are you going to do?
You must repent, however, you have not sought forgiveness,

Jesus said, "And to that I'd be a witness,
Open your heart and mind, search it well, then seek forgiveness.
All it requires is willingness."

1 Chronicles 28:9

Know thou the God of thy father and serve him with a perfect heart and with a willing mind: for the Lord searcheth all hearts, and understandeth all the imaginations of the thoughts: if thou seek him, he will be found of thee; but if thou forsake him, he will cast thee off for ever.

The Shepherd

When we stay in touch with God,
We don't trod on unfamiliar sod!
When we hear His voice,
We know that it is He, so we rejoice!
In a soft and gentle way,
He leads us each day.

But, when we stray away from Him,
That soft and gentle way, turns into a firm tug.
Because it is you and I He really loves!

Have you ever been around A Shepherd and His sheep?
For the one sheep who wanders away,
The Shepherd breaks his leg.
Then, The Shepherd throws him over His shoulders,
And carries him all the way,
Just to keep him from going astray.

Isaiah 53:6

All we like sheep have gone astray, We have turned everyone to his own way; And the Lord hath laid on him the iniquity of us all.

To the Realm Of Confusion

I was soaring to the realm of confusion,
Sometimes even faced with the sight of an optical illusion.
Then with a sudden burst of revelation,
I came to the conclusion,
It was Satan at the head of all that mind-boggling confusion!
The master of confusion is confused, because this battle,
he is losing!

Greater is He that is in me.
I know The Holy Spirit is what freed me!
All Satan can do is lay eyes on me,
Through the fluttering of a band of Angel's wings!
Until the golden bell rings!

With the hedge of protection all around,
Satan, it is back to Hell where you're bound!
In the continuous ring of fire, no Christians will be found!
Dear Christian Soldiers, always keep your knees on the ground,
Because when in constant prayer, the realm of confusion cannot be found!

1 Corinthians 14:33
For God is not the author of confusion, but of peace, as in all churches of saints.

Don't Risk It

We cannot allow our Bibles to become dusty,
For it is then all God's commands become rusty.

When rust builds on metal it causes it to break.
That would mean spiritual death, a risk we can't afford to take.

God's commands must stay fresh on our mind.
Staying fresh on our mind is the only way to stay out of a bind.

God's commands keep us in a square frame,
All of which keep us from feeling guilty and going insane,

Not to mention becoming spiritually lame.

Romans 8:6
For to be carnally minded is death; but to be spiritually minded is life and peace.

Praises unto God

Father, I want to sing praises unto You,
For Your love is ever true.

The praises that I sing are coming from my heart.
My heart was vexed unclean until Your miracle took part.

You came in, cleansing and removing all sin and pain.
Now, a melodious joy exists because Your love doth remain.

I give praises unto You, for Your love doth renew.
It delivered me from despair, giving hope to all I do.

I sing with joy unto You, Father God,
As I prayerfully endure my journey on earthly sod.

I can't wait to enter Heaven's Gate.
All Saints will be singing praises unto You on any given date.

Father God, You are Holy and Magnificent.
Perpetual singing of praises unto You is prayerfully sufficient.

Father God, I love and adore You.
I pleasantly seek to know more of You.

Isaiah 60:18

Violence shall no more be heard in thy land, wasting nor destruction within thy borders; but thou shalt call thy walls Salvation, and thy gates Praise.

Prayer Time

God designed prayer time for us to mentally and physically unwind.
He wanted us to be able to communicate
and relieve our worries and stress anytime.

Time in prayer is well spent and we waste plenty of that stressed-out with worries on our mind.
We all think we have no time to spare, but time spent in worry, can be spared your time.

No time spent in prayer to our Heavenly Father
is a waste of our time.
Must we be reminded, He gives us all of our time?

Our time spent in prayer can take place anywhere,
Standing or sitting or lying.
Isn't it amazing how much time we can spare?

So the moment you begin to worry,
turn your worry into prayer.
You will be amazed to see the positive results
from just one moment spared to prayer!

Daniel 9:17
Now therefore, O our God, hear the prayer of thy servant, and his supplications, and cause thy face to shine upon thy sanctuary that is desolate, for the Lord's sake.

SILENCE

It is in silence
God gives guidance.

This world is so full of noise with great elements of violence,
Not enough time given to silence.

It is God's voice we must hear.
It is His message that would relieve all fear.

Stop the music! Turn off the television and the video!
Kneel in prayer. Tune in to God's Show.

After praise and repentance, just listen.
If you don't, you will never know your mission.

In taking time to pray
You are allowing God to show you the way.

You will be amazed, what The Master has to say,
Said directly to you in His special way.

You are blessed! So be on your way.
You just sent the devil back to hell today
Simply when you knelt to pray!

Luke 18:1
And he spake a parable unto them to this end, that men ought to always pray, and not to faint;

Power of Prayer

Imagine the power in one hour of prayer . . .
Look at the miracles that happened in an instant.

No it's not magic, it's realistic.
There is no need to try and justify.

Miracles in their miraculous way can alone testify.
Because God is so good! His miracles cannot be misunderstood.

Enjoy the splendor and Thank Jesus for He is the Mender.
And Thank God, He is the Sender.

The recipients of miracles are not pretenders.

1 John 1:6
If we say that we have fellowship with Him and walk in darkness, we lie, and do not the truth.

Humble Pie

Have you tried a slice of humble pie?
It is out of this world, and it's falling from the sky.

Served straight from Heaven, God's style;
Served not for just one, but for all who walk the aisle.

Servings are free; don't open your wallet, it's not money you need,
But an open mind and heart to obey His call, so you can heed.

It really was not free; because of the cross He did bleed.
A choice offer, knowing humility and salvation
is our greatest need.

So help yourself to a big serving.
Advance notice: this piece will be napkin-deserving.

This serving will bring tears of joy.
It will be removing pride before you; let it destroy.

The only way it is served is on bended knee.
That is serving humility with style, in humble reverence just for thee.

Make no mistake!
That's "humble pie," and it's great!

Psalms 9:12
When he maketh inquisition for blood, he remembereth them: he forgetteth not the cry of the humble.

I'm Not Alone

Because You came to me,
I could no longer hide from thee!

Now my wayward ways are gone,
And I Thank God I am no longer alone!

Oh Sweet Savior, You are always at my side,
Since the best day of my life, when I put away my foolish pride.

I am so thankful that I met and know You,
It is in you whom I know I can confide.

Thank You for removing my foolish pride,
For now it is in you, whom I, will forever abide.

Always knowing I'm not alone!

Colossians 2:6–7 (NIV)

So then, just as you received Christ Jesus as Lord, continue to live in Him, rotted and built up in Him, strengthened in the faith as you were taught, and over-flowing with thankfulness.

My Foolish Pride

My foolish pride is what kept me in the dark.
The sins of the past and the sin I was living in was leaving its mark.
Putting away my pride, meant to self I must die.
I was dying inside; so I thought at that point, I'd give anything a try.

Why, oh why, did I wait so long; that was the best decision ever,
after all the games I played.
God was patiently waiting to redeem what He had made.
I tried every single day to forget about Him.
But I was His creation, one of the Master's pieces,
and He doesn't forget about them.

He truly wants us to confide in Him,
Then only realizing, we should always rely upon Him.
Now there is such comfort in knowing God abides in me.
My dear Savior, thanks for removing my foolish pride.

I am so glad I didn't listen to all of Satan's foolish lies.

Proverbs 8:13 (NIV)
To fear the Lord is to hate evil; I hate pride and arrogance, evil behavior and perverse speech.

REDEMPTION

A New Heart

Tears can heal your broken heart,
If from a humbled heart they did start.
When we break to self,
He takes us off the shelf.

Wipes us clean,
All new it seems, what a dream.
He gives us a new start,
It is His wisdom, He doth impart.

With a new heart,
We can do our part.
Pray, He'll direct thy way.
Pray His will, for within His will we must stay!

Psalms 34:18

The Lord is nigh unto them that are of a broken heart; and saveth such as be of a contrite Spirit.

Stressful

If the way we live our life is stressful,
Don't you think everyone else can tell?
Maybe it has been a bit too long since on our knees we've fell.

It's not just the unusual stress
That makes our life a complete mess.
It is our sins, in which we forget to confess.

Go to the Father, truly seeking His forgiveness;
His blessings are freely given to each and everyone of us.
It's in His arms we are peacefully assured,
He is in control, removing our stress!

That would be stress-less living at its best.

Mark 11:25–26

And when you stand praying, forgive, if ye have ought against any: that your Father also which is in Heaven may forgive you your trespasses. But if ye do not forgive, neither will your Father which is in Heaven forgive your trespasses.

A Hungry World

In our world today ever increasing is hunger, not just for nutritional substance.
We are starving for acceptance, forgiveness, and gratification that comes only through repentance.

This starvation can only be broken
By the acceptance of God's love token.

God's token of love is His Son Jesus.
God's Son Jesus is the only one who can truly free us.

We must accept Jesus as the Son of God, and as our Lord and Savior.
We must give God the praise, for He removed our unacceptable behavior.

We are no longer left to spiritual starvation.
For our soul's hunger is replenished by God for the duration.

Psalms 107:9

For He satisfieth the longing soul, and filleth the hungry soul with goodness.

Out of Control

My life was ever changing, simply out of control!
What was my future to hold?
No peace! No rest!
Just burdens that made me depressed!

I had always been told there was a Man to behold.
My doubt! My fear!
Told me He was nowhere near!
With my shame and sadness, I was sending out signals of SOS.

Whatever contentment is? It must be found!
I must get off this tiring merry-go-round!
I fell to my knees.
I cried Father, forgive me, please!

At that moment He took control,
Restoring me and making me WHOLE!

Psalms 23:3
He restoreth my soul: he leadeth me in the paths of righteousness for his name's sake.

In Need of Refreshing

Envy will destroy you and your ability.
It takes you away from all reality.

The fact that you are totally capable
Escapes you, making you believe that you are truly incapable.

Envy causes your beauty to disappear in this case.
Envy gives you the gift of harsh lines on your face.

Your stable emotional state slowly melts, leaving you a basket case.
Turn from Envy and trust in God. Then, the harsh lines will be erased.

God will refresh you with His Love by Grace.
His Love leaves the gift of His beauty tactfully in place.

His love wipes away envy leaving no scars to trace.
No longer allowing Envy to cause you total disgrace.

Father God, Thank You for Your Love and Saving Grace.

Acts 3:19 (NIV)
Repent then turn to God, so that your sins may be wiped out, that times of refreshing come from the Lord.

Life Ain't No Game

Life is no longer the same
Since I called upon your name.

I was tired and growing weary from playing life as if game.
I was rapidly going madly insane.

Your Holy Spirit spoke to my heart, questioning why I was living in shame?
I had heard most all of my life I could call upon Your name.

I thought briefly to myself, this wild and broken heart, Jesus must tame.
It took Your amazing Grace to pardon my sins and erase all the shame.

Your Love showed me Your gift called Life, certainly ain't no game!
I thank God, in Jesus Name.

Colossians 1:21–22 (NAS)
Yet He has now reconciled you in His fleshly body through death, in order to present you before Him holy and blameless and beyond reproach.

No Other Way

Do you smile?
Do you walk that extra mile?
If someone had to take a wild guess,
Would they see Jesus in you or is your life a complete mess?
Now is the time to confess,
Did you really invite Him into your heart to stay?
Or did you just come to the altar to make a hypocritical display?

If need be, you better get it straight today.
Let God show you the way.

If God's leadership is to your dismay,
You must let self get out of the way!

Just invite Jesus into your heart today.
And be aware for Satan will try to lead you astray!

You must read The Bible and pray everyday,
For my friend, there is certainly no other way!

Proverbs 15:13 (NIV)

A happy heart makes the face cheerful, but heartache crushes the spirit.

Most Adored

My strength comes from you, Lord.
My sincere apology, for so long it was you that I ignored.

Now you are first in my life, and You are most adored.
I read The Bible daily in hopes that every word in my heart is stored.

I prayerfully give all Thanks,
and in song I sing praises to you, Dear Lord.
You alone are most worthy of all praises and must be adored.

Not only do you give the gifts
of Forgiveness, Hope, Love and Grace . . .
You also give our souls a forever, resting place.

Thank You, for preparing me to see You face to face.
"Wow" that is abundant Grace!

Isaiah 41:6 (NIV)
Each helps the other and says to his brother, "Be strong!"

Common Place

The Christian family is Satan's most commonplace
For him to invite himself in just to show disgrace.

If you open the window to sin,
That is giving him the signal to let himself in.

Satan is like a big hyper dog
That has not been on his daily jog.

He knocks you to the ground by sudden surprise
Before you even have time to blink your eyes.

He tells you sin is more enjoyable than it is. He lies!
When we start listening to him,
our family broken-heartedly cries!

In Heaven, Satan before God, had one too many lies to tell.
That's why God cast him into a burning Hell!

Close all your windows of sinful opportunity.
They are all personal invitations from him!
Then, Satan with his deadly deception cannot enter in.

Don't let his deception mislead you into sin.
When you accept Jesus as your Savior, just call upon Him.

At that very moment Satan is defeated. He will never win.
Jesus is conqueror against Satan every time, My friend,
until the very end!

Romans 8:37 (NIV)
No, in all things we are more than conquerors through Him that loved us.

BEWARE MY FRIEND

Watch your travel, my friend,
All those places you frequently go;
Would they invite Jesus in?
If not, beware, my friend,
You should not enter in.
All you will find in there
Is bitterness,
Rage and anger,
Creating much danger,
Because to Satan
You are a stranger!

They will surely recognize
in you
Our Savior through your behavior.
Because, with Him,
Kindness, love, joy and compassion
Will shine through you
And evil is just waiting to attack you!
Just remember,
When confusion's in the air,
Satan's in the midst.

James 4:4 (NIV)
Anyone who chooses to be a friend of the world is hatred toward God.

Deceiver Relieved of Duty

We must not forget,
It was Satan
Whom God did relieve . . .

Satan is always trying to get even by constantly deceiving.
He is evil and is always seeking revenge.

Satan cannot succeed
Because it was God's word he did not heed.
He is full of wicked deeds,
And at the weak he unrelentingly pleads.
He tries to make them believe sin will satisfy their deepest needs.

Just remember what God has control of
Heart, Mind, Body and Soul;
Satan and all the demons of hell cannot take control of.
Jesus came to Save, Redeem and Cleanse us,
And to remove the skims from our eyes
so we can recognize Satan's evil deeds.

By the act of a simple prayer of rebuke, in The Name of Jesus,
the great deceiver flees.
You are now informed it is only Jesus from our sin and danger who frees,
And it is He who will satisfy our greatest needs.
"Come unto me and I will give you rest" that is how He pleads.

Proverbs 14:8

The wisdom of the prudent is to understand his way: but the folly of fools is deceit.

Private Life

Living our lives in a private way
Is turning out to be a sinful hide-away.

Living privately in sin by the big and small
Is exactly what will turn out to be our nation's fall.

Living in a private way should be fine
As long as we walk God's straight and narrow line.

When we let the Bible get dusty
Our spiritual life becomes rusty.

Therefore, it becomes most difficult to see the line
Between good and bad. Life becomes crazy all the time.

The important things in life
constantly slip our mind.
Somehow your company seems to grow with the lost kind.

Unfortunately your soul, like theirs, will slip in Hell's front line.
So, Dear one, don't you think it's time to change
the way you spend your private time?

Hurry up, and get back on track.
For this is the only way to conquer Satan's attack.

Psalms 5:8

Lead me, O Lord, in thy righteousness because of mine enemies; make thy ways straight before my face.

Caught Up

Are you caught up in the glare of the glamorous things in the world?
Are you tiring in your search for earthy pleasures and great treasures?

See God's Blessings. You can't count them—they're beyond measure.

I don't think you have knowledge of your need for a Savior.
It definitely shows by the looks of your behavior.

You go about your way freely not accepting the gift of God's Grace.
It's not hard to see you bear no fruit of the Holy Spirit—not a trace.

The Holy Spirit reveals hurt, which has caused unbelief.
Turning to God is the only way to find relief.

Stop in The Name of Our Lord Jesus and save yourself much grief.
By the acceptance, repentance, and belief, salvation happens in a brief.

Why do we waste the major part of our lives?

Neglecting His Law of commands for which they stand.
Rejecting His Love and extended hand.
Grieving over our past.
How long will you let it last?

Mark 9:24

And straightway the father of the child cried out, and said with tears, Lord, I believe; help thou mine unbelief.

Pleasure Seeking

The madness in seeking pleasure is life threatening.
No pleasure is found in your search alone. It's frightening.

Pleasure is not bought at any cost,
When your heart and soul is lost.

Allow me to inform you, so you are aware,
It was Jesus Christ who paid our fare.

No peace or pleasure will you ever find
Until you lay your sins on God's forgiveness line. It's divine!

That is what God had in mind, total submission of our life.
Or
Hell on Earth, and for all Eternity too, that is inconceivable strife.

Through redemption, peace emerges in the giving of new life,
Giving the word pleasure, a new meaning to our redeemed life.

The greatest pleasure is the peace received through rebirth,
Making life a more pleasurable experience while here on earth.

Ezekiel 18:23
Have I any pleasure at all that the wicked should die? Saith the Lord God: and not that he should return from his ways, and live?

A Sin Not to Share

To the one, most dare not speak,
They are the ones we must seek.
Their lives are so incomplete,
Without Jesus they will never be complete.
They are lost and undone,
Because our mission we have not done.
Don't forget He gave His only son,
That is how the mission was begun.
Just a little of your time given to Him,
So these hurting people can receive Him.
Just your time that you would be giving; not bad.
For He gave all He had.
It should be A Crime, not just a sin, not to share,
His message, so they can be spared.
You see their pain.
In their shoes, would you want to remain?
Must I continue to explain?
Unless you share the word,
In pain, they'll remain.
Because they will spend their eternity in Hell too!

2 Peter 3:9

The Lord is not slack concerning his promise, as some men count slackness; but is longsuffering to us-ward, not willing that any should perish, but that all should come to repentance.

Calling All Saints

If you are feeling kind of faint,
Then it's on your knees, you ain't.

What kind of a picture must God paint?
Can't you see it's your spirituality that Satan is trying to taint!

Go to the Savior and ask Him to strengthen you.
So you can do what He has called you to do.

To seek the lost,
At all cost.

Just hold on to the Savior's hand, and there will be no confusion.
Only the strength of the Holy Spirit of God, a spiritual transfusion!

The final conclusion:
For your mission is, only the faint are losing.

And it is the faint that God is not using!

Isaiah 40:31

But they that wait upon the Lord shall renew their strength; they shall mount up with wings as eagles, they shall run, and not be weary, and they shall, and not faint.

At Your Feet I Rest

I like myself best
Since at Your feet I rest.

No evil can stand ground
With You all around.

That which was an old stronghold
Can't take control,

All because it's Your hand I hold.
Father, You help me to be bold,
When temptation tries . . .
To grab hold!

You are always there to remind me,

My peace,
My soul,
Can't be bought or sold.

Nahum 1:7

The Lord is Good, a strong hold in the day of trouble; and He knoweth them that trust in Him.

Energy

I was feeling depleted of all my energy,
Not knowing what my body needed.
It was then His Word I heeded.

"Come unto me, all of ye who are weary, and I will give you rest."

This was not a spiritual test.
It was me that was blessed.

My Faith increased,
My Mind was cleared,
My load was lifted,
My Strength restored,

Supplication from Our Savior, whom I Adore.

Psalms 23:3
He restoreth my soul: He leadeth me in the paths of righteousness for His name's sake.

Matthew 11:29
Take my yoke upon you, and learn of me; for I am meek and lowly in heart: and ye shall find rest unto your souls.

Fear of the Unknown

The fears of what might be in our future – of the unknown creep in.
Thank God, only momentarily, for God's peace is within.

Satan cannot steal our peace with his fearful ploy.
God's peace is there and He replaces the fear with joy.

We may be physically alone;
But, Dear, if by choice we are God's Child,
remember, He is still on the Throne.

He makes His presence well-known, when to Him we pray.
He is there to lead and guide us every step of the way.

There is peace available to all in the busy city.
There is peace to have in the country too, even for those living in pity.

Heavenly Father, I know it is all because of You,
For I lived in constant fear, no peace within, all before I met you.

Now my daily prayer is for You to lead me to assist those
who live in constant fear.

Isaiah 41:10 (NIV)

Fear not, for I am with you; be not dismayed, for I am your God. I will strengthen you, yes, I will help you, I will uphold you with my righteous right hand.

He Is Listening

Sad and pitiful is the individual who let's God pass them by.
Saddened by attempts for you to meet Him,
you didn't even acknowledge His earnest cry.

Now, as the time has come and you're about to die,
You lay there looking out the window into God's beautiful sky.

You now question your own decisions of the past,
When sadly, you recognize with a terrible blast!
Our earthly life don't last.

Your Heavenly Father is waiting to hear your desperate cry,
He truly understands you, for it was He who made you
a smart guy.

However, being secularly knowledgeable, is only worldly smart,
That, dear one, in Heaven plays no part!

You must go to the Father through His Son, as innocent
as a child, and
repent from your heart.
Then, my dear, even though late in life, you played out your part.

Giving God your broken heart, all burdened with sin,
Before out of this world you depart, gives you eternal life with no end.

Praise The Lord, For Great is His Faithfulness, unto us.
He left this brief message only to prepare us.

1 Thessalonians 5:2
For yourselves know perfectly that the day of the Lord so cometh as a thief in the night.

Burning Desire

Now my burning desire, is my yearning for You.
No longer feeling that empty void, for my heart is filled
with Your Love True.
Your spiritual anointing is continually flowing.
The peace that is overflowing is just Your Love that is now showing.

Father, please send me, for I am willing to go.
Wherever I am needed, to carry out Your Will, please show.

Seeking the fallen for their needs are dire,
This has always been Your Mission, and to that I aspire.

Give me what is needed to be on the way.
Your Holy Spirit's anointing is needed for each step of the way.

No matter if it's night or day, I pray
for your guidance from above,
Please Father cover my weaknesses in order
to radiate Your pure Love.
Already knowing that Love is what they need the most,
Father, I pray to be like You, a Gracious Host.

Ecclesiastes 3:8

A time to love, and a time to hate; a time of war, and a time of peace.

TIMING IS EVERYTHING

You must not be caught a second without
God the Father, Son and Holy Spirit.
It's Hell, if you're caught without, them.

In the event you do not know,
You must accept Jesus as God's Son;
Or it's Hell for you, where time has no end.

My Dear Friend, don't believe Satan's lies.
Timing is everything until one dies.
Dying to sin, instantly spiritual life begins,

Allowing the Trinity to enter in.
There is no time greater than the releasing of sins.
The Spiritual Clock for your lost soul ends!

Satan was cheating you of time with Christ.
I'm glad you didn't need time to think twice.
It's Heaven, when your time is spent wise.

Timing Is Everything.
If you miss your timely call,
You would have had the worst timing of all.

Making the time Jesus spent on The Cross,
For your soul's salvation
A total loss!

Revelation 20:15

And whosoever was not found written in the book of life was cast into the lake of fire.

In the Nick of Time

Behind our broken heart's door stands deep pain,
accompanied with great sorrow.
There have been many days that we have even prayed
for no tomorrow.
Denial is a constant state of mind, denial of our life being
in God's master plan.
We are very fortunate that God's master plan still stands.

With our heart's door firmly closed,
there's no view of who we are supposed to be in You.
But in the Master's plan,
God Himself opens a window with a magnificent view.
Standing all the while behind the firmly closed door
of our broken heart . . .
Is
Hope, Peace, Joy, and His unconditional abundant Love . . .
Personally sent from our Heavenly Father God, up above.

God always sends us just what we need,
By intercession of the Holy Spirit,
Just in "the nick of time!"

Romans 15:13 (NAS)

Now may the God of hope fill you with all joy and peace in believing, that you may abound in hope by the power of the Holy Spirit.

Ten Percent

Don't waste your time
Trying to make an extra dime.
Cause if you're not giving your full ten percent,
It won't be very long until you haven't a cent.

You must not forget, 'twas God only who lent.
That's just in case you haven't a hint.
That's a valuable message from God The Father.
He does not want to harp, or even a bother.

So, for all your time wasted and His money spent,
You must now repent!
It was all extravagantly spent in vain.
Not even your ten percent was spent in Jesus' name.

Genesis 28:22

And this stone, which I have set for a pillar, shall be God's house: and of all that thou shalt give me will surely give the tenth unto thee.

Free

By the blood of Jesus, we are no longer bound to the sins of our past.
Jesus our Lord and Savior has removed them at last.
Satan and all his demons are continuously trying to harass,
But we are no longer bound to him.
Our dear Savior freed us from all that trash.

We've all been afraid, people would point their fingers and
laugh, forgetting what they have done.
However, they too must look in the mirror
and see who's laughing,
for they must look beyond
The blood of Jesus . . . to see the forgiven sins of our past.
For our dear Savior has freed us at last.

They must not know they must remove
the skims from their eyes,
Before their time is up and their sinful self dies.
Satan wants to take their lost soul
where the foolish man forever cries.
But by the blood of Jesus the repented will not go there,
Jesus freed us from hell's cries.

The truth of whom we used to be
Before repentance can no longer continue to haunt you and me.
For our dear Savior knows the confessed truth.

For He is the Truth and the Truth is He.
And the Truth has set us free.

Thankful to God we will forever be,
For it was He who sent His Son for sinners, such as you and me!

John 8:31b–32

If you continue in my word, then are ye my disciples indeed; And ye shall know the truth, and the truth shall make you free.

Provision

Prayerfully, must we be reminded
that it is a sin to be blinded to Your love undue?
For anything we say or do that is negative
cast clouds of doubt to what's true.

Your Love and Grace are truly amazing;
therefore, no doubts can linger on.
In the same manner, your patience and provision,
while in deepest doubt, continue on.

When reoccurring thoughts of doubt creep in,
we must realize this is a sin.
It is a very humbling experience when we realize
Jesus was always there within.

The Holy Spirit provides exactly what we need, but we must allow.
God will confront all doubt with His promises,
Starting with the here and now.

Psalm 85:10
Mercy and Truth are met together; righteousness and peace have kissed each other.

Apostate

To know the Love and Amazing Grace of God,
Then allow the entanglements of sin to pollute them, seem odd?

The apostle Paul told us in Hebrews to hold steadfast to Faith.
Entanglement with sin leads to death for The Lord Saith.

It is better to have not known the way of righteousness
Than to have known the way and then turn to ungodliness.

The commandments of God were written in love.
The only way to escape from death's grip is to turn to God above.

All sinfulness begins with thoughts that come to mind.
Carnal mindedness is Satan's ploy for enmity against God's mind.

You cannot go back to the entanglements of sin and strife,
For there is no renunciation of the sacrifice of Jesus Christ's life,
Or
You will forfeit the gift from God . . .
Called Eternal Life.

Hebrews 10:26
For if we sin willfully after we have received the knowledge of the truth, there remaineth no more sacrifice for sins.

Activist for Christ

I know whom I serve and have placed all my belief in.
I know whom I have placed all my trust and faith in.

My smile reflects my Savior, Jesus Christ and His love for me.
My life after redemption reflects my love for He.

No matter great or small,
Nothing is below or beyond Him. He is interested in them all.

I must share the good news of the Gospel of Jesus Christ,
In sharing it, let them know it is imperative that all must be born twice,

Acceptance by faith, that Jesus is God's Son.
Then, my Dear One, half the battle is won.

In Confessing, along with the repentance of your sin,
The Placement of trust is a must turning to full reliance upon Him.

Peace and pleasure comes naturally as your new life begins.
This is a gift of the Holy Spirit you, too, can share with friends.

There are many ways to be an "Activist for Christ."
I personally feel the best is telling the lost, we must all be born twice.

1 Peter 1:22–23

Seeing ye have purified your souls in obeying the truth through the Spirit unto unfeigned love of the brethren, see that ye love one another with a pure heart fervently: Being born against, not of corruptible seed, but of incorruptible, by the word of God, which liveth and abideth for ever.

Crowded Place

Have you ever been in a crowded public place
Without seeing smiles on anybody's face?

That is almost unbelievable to me.
They're all in need of Amazing Grace from He.

How many people could it be?
Amazing Grace is free, and it's for you and me.

We may never know how this could be.
God uses all, that includes you and me.

We are to minister to lost souls and hurting hearts.
I dare not ask if we are actively doing our parts.

Proverbs 14:25

A true witness delivereth souls: but a deceitful witness speaketh lies.

Leadership

To be a leader,
You must be a reader
Of God's Holy and true word.

For there is no other way,
His word is our guide, and it is here to stay.
It is the only true guide for leaders in the past and for today.

So don't be overwhelmed or get carried away,
When others think they know a better way.
Just go to your Bible and God will show you the only successful way.

Now you must be on your God instructed way,
Showing others
How God's Holy word can bless them in the same way.

Deuteronomy 32:12
So the Lord alone did lead him, and there was no strange god with him.

Stop Being Stubborn

Stop being stubborn and unyielding to Christ.
You have heard it said, one must be born twice.

Holding your thoughts to yourself and trying to be nice,
Won't get you to Heaven, so you'd better think twice.

You must accept, repent, and believe
Before into the family of God, you can be received.

After asking to be forgiven,
My Dear, that is when in life you begin living.

Freed from the bondage of sin,
There will never be a battle that you can't win.

Psalms 32:9

Be ye not as the horse, or as the mule, which have no understanding: whose mouth must be held in with a bit and bridle, lest they come near unto thee.

Tired of Starting Over

If you're tired of starting over,
Give it up and turn it over.

Give up your sin to Jesus, He is the only one
who can let us truly start over.
Tell the devil you are no longer playing Red Rover.

Giving up our sin,
Gives us victory over sin and sorrow, that's only through Him.
The Victory for us, an eternal story, that has no end!

Starting over without Him,
A battle that would ultimately be a deadly sin;
Without Jesus, sin is a battle you cannot win!

1 John 5:3-4
For this is the love of God, that we keep his commandments: and his commandments are not grievous. For whatsoever is born of God overcometh the world: and this is the victory that overcometh the world, even in our faith.

Be Ye Transformed

Being truthfully transformed,
Is humanly impossible!
However, it is a miracle that only God can perform.

From a sinner to a saint,
That is something not even an artist could paint.

It's victory through His Son, Jesus we can claim,
For we no longer have to carry our shame.

We are freed from sins, bondage and pain,
For Jesus cleansed all our stain.

We must remember it is Satan,
Just lying in wait to attack.

We must go to our knees,
And put on the full armor of God for our protection.

For the armor of God is the only way we can send Satan running
in the opposite direction.
With forgiveness of sin, eternal life, and wearing new armored attire,
that's transformation!

Romans 12:2

Be not conformed to this world: but be ye transformed by the renewing of your mind, that ye may prove what is that good, and acceptable, and perfect, will of God.

Wisdom Abounds

When wisdom abounds,
Satan in all his stupidity drowns.
Time for a reality check; don't let your soul with the devil's drown.

Humble yourself before the Heavenly Father
by going to your knees,
Asking the Father to help you, please,
Giving,
Wisdom, Peace,
and Love, . . .
Which truly comes from God above.

No earthly institution
gives wisdom, . . .
Which is only truly given by God, without any confusion.

No drink or substance
gives peace . . .
Forever.
Only God's peace passeth all understanding.

No being on earth
gives love . . .
Without many varying conditions.

For God so loved the world He gave His only Son.

We shall give Him thanks for His profound wisdom,
before each giving day has begun!
We shall not forget Satan in his stupidity drowns.

Proverbs 2:6

For the Lord giveth wisdom: out of his mouth cometh knowledge and understanding.

Don't Be a Fool

It wasn't on Jesus I was trying to depend.
In fact, I didn't give much time to Him.

I had lost track of all the sin I was allowing to creep in,
After all, it was just a little, now and then.

All sin no matter how big or little,
unfortunately, it separates us from Him.
We can't be fooled, we must ask forgiveness for our sin,
not just disregard them.

A sin-filled life is wide open for more hurt,
We must realize our soul with death, is being a flirt.

After realization, my friend;
It is only on Jesus, I now depend!

Proverbs 28:26 (NIV)
He who trusts in himself is a fool. But he who walks in wisdom is kept safe.

Peer Pressure

Do not rebel. Be polite, kind and courageous.
Your actions among your peers will be very contagious.

You must first seek The Kingdom of God.
God is The Creator of all, in the sea and on earthly sod.

Carefully obey God's commands with strong conviction.
Your peers will see first-hand God's Love and Strength are for real, not fiction!

Be leaders to The Cross for Christ's sake,
Creating genuine Love, not fake.

Got Jesus?

That's all it takes!

Proverbs 4:5, 23 (NLT)
Learn to be wise and develop good judgment . . . Above all else, guard your heart, for it affects everything you do.

Performance of Light

The severe storms on earth may rage.
You must not forget God is in control. He is setting the stage.
As the lightning bolts across the scene of the dark sky,
Remember, this scene too, is from God on high.

This is how God appears in the midst of our dark sin-filled heart.
It is His Love, Hope and Wisdom in an instant He doth impart,
Saving our soul, calming our emotions that raged out of control.
Proper placement of heart and soul gives us a new earthly role.

We must be responsible and tell the Salvation story
Of The Savior's Love that gives us Eternal life in Glory.
With the saving light's strike, brings the performance of new life,
Being viewed center stage by God, Christians and the lost alike.

The basic lines for our performance can only be found
In "THE BOOK OF LIFE." The Truth in the lines is profound.
It takes a repenting heart to fulfill our role,
Always leaving "THE MASTER" in control.

Job 28:26-28

When He made a decree for the rain, and a way for the lightning of the thunder: Then He did see it, and declare it; He prepared it, yea, and searched it out. And unto man He said, Behold, the fear of the Lord, that is wisdom; and to depart from evil is understanding.

A Survivor

When you are abused, you are stuck between a rock and a hard place.
It is not about the color of your skin or origin of race.
It is complexly, a miserable place,

Trying to keep up the pace;
Always trying to maintain a pleasant looking face.
Underneath the mask, always feeling like a total disgrace.

God helped me, and He will help you, too.
First, you must ask for direction in all you do.
No fax, cell or lan-line will do.

It is a direct, open prayer line to connect you
To God The Father. He is the only one who will deliver you.
He left you this message, but you must follow through.

Jeremiah 33:3
Call unto me, and I will answer thee, and shew thee great and mighty things, which thou knowest not.

Envy

Envy will destroy you and your ability.
It takes you away from all reality.

The fact that you are totally capable
Escapes you, making you believe that you are totally incapable.

Envy causes your beauty to disappear, in this case.
Envy gives you the gift of harsh lines upon your face.

Your stable, emotional state slowly melts, leaving you a basket case.
Turn from envy and trust in God, then all harsh lines will be erased.

God will refresh you with His love by grace;
His Love leaves the gift of His beauty, tactfully in place.

His love wipes away envy, leaving no scars to trace.
No longer allowing envy to cause you disgrace.

Father God, thank You for Your love and saving grace.

Job 5:2
For wrath killeth the foolish man, and envy slayeth the silly one.

SINNER'S PRAYER

Dear God,

I am Lost.
I am a Sinner.
Please forgive me,
Of my sins,
Please save me,
Take control of my life.
Have mercy on me,
I ask in Jesus name and for His sake.
You are my only Hope of Salvation.
Amen!

Matthew 9:13

For I am not come to call the righteous, but the sinners to repentance.

Acts 26:18

To open their eyes, and to turn them from darkness to light, and from the power of Satan unto God, that they may receive forgiveness of sins, and inheritance among them which are sanctified by faith that is in me

To order additional copies of

My Peace, My Soul...

Can't Be Bought or Sold

Have your credit card ready and call

toll free **(877) 421-READ (7323)**

or send $13.95* each plus $4.95 S&H**

to

WinePress Publishing
PO Box 428
Enumclaw, WA 98022

www.winepresspub.com

*WA residents, add 8.4% sales tax

**Add $1.00 S&H for each additional book ordered.